# Churches
## of
# Shropshire

Lawrence Garner

A small token of gratitude for all your kindness.

Love. Charlotte.

*Shropshire Books*

Front Cover: St. Eata's, Atcham. Photograph by Gordon Dickins.

Back Cover: East window of the south aisle at Moreton Corbet.
Photograph by David George.



ISBN: 0-903802-59-7

Cover and book design: Daywell Designs

Drawings: Kathryn Green

Managing Editor: Helen Sample

Published by Shropshire Books, the publishing division of the
Leisure Services Department of Shropshire County Council.

Printed by Liveseys Ltd.

# Acknowledgements

The publishers wish to thank the following for their kind permission to reproduce photographs in this book: Peter Criddle, p95; The Royal Commission on the Historical Monuments of England, p52; David George, back cover; Gordon Dickins, front cover; Lawrence Garner,pp3, 6, 10, 15, 62, 97, 102, 104, 126; the remaining photographs are from Shropshire County Council's Records and Research Deaprtment.

# About the Author

Lawrence Garner has lived in Shropshire for over twenty years, and for ten of them was a teacher in Oswestry. In 1980 he decided to leave the teaching profession for a new career as an author and journalist, and has written on landscape and countryside topics for the Financial Times, Daily Telegraph and Guardian and for a variety of magazines.

For three years he was Director of the Dry Stone Walling Association, and as a result became a practising waller, a trade which he was only recently persuaded to abandon by the onset of rheumatism. However, he still teaches the craft, and his book *Dry Stone Walls* for Shire Publications is a standard work.

He is the author of guidebooks to the Welsh Border, the Severn and Avon, Shropshire and Gwynedd, but his specialist field is architecture, and a comprehensive study of Shropshire architecture has already resulted in two volumes of the *Buildings of Shropshire* series, covering the period from 1580 to 1840.

He is currently working on a book of personal reminiscences of growing up in his native county of Sussex.

# Contents

# FOREWORD

Parish churches have a unique place in the hearts of most English people. Even those who pay scant regard to their spiritual function regard them as an essential feature of our heritage, and will react fiercely if their own local church is threatened with closure, let alone demolition.

The reality is that every church is an expensive luxury that has to be paid for, and in most cases the responsibility lies with a small minority of worshippers within each parish. The popular belief that churches are maintained by the Church Commissioners or supported out of public funds is wrong. Only buildings of exceptional architectural value can expect to receive outside help with repairs. The fact is that the problem of keeping our churches in existence becomes ever more desperate, especially when buildings become redundant - and redundancy will become increasingly common as the Church of England is forced to speed up its rationalisation of the parish system.

Yet the public belief that churches should be sacrosanct remains strong. The inescapable conclusion is that many much-loved buildings are destined to be converted or demolished unless far more people are prepared to contribute to their costs, either directly or through taxes. But the principle of supporting churches out of public funds is fraught with controversy, in spite of the fact that many churches are major tourist attractions.

In fact there is a very good case for preserving these buildings even if they are no longer needed, because the parish churches of England represent one of the most important strands in our architectural history - and in our social history too. What is more, they are uniquely accessible. You may have to travel many miles to visit an important Norman castle or Elizabethan house, but if you have a car you can trace the development of church building styles from Romanesque to Edwardian in the course of a single day, no matter where you live. And church visitors' books show that more and more people are taking advantage of the fact.

Hence this book, which is primarily an attempt to show how the churches of Shropshire reflect the history of English architecture. The secondary purpose is to point out that remote or unassuming churches have an equal right to be considered a valuable part of our building history. Each one is loved by its congregation, but that will not be enough, and I hope that the book will not only open up a little more of the riches that lie just beyond our doorsteps but raise the question of how much longer they are likely to be there for us to enjoy.

The first part of this book is a survey of church building in the county up to the late Victorian period, while in the second part I have selected forty churches for more detailed consideration, treating them not only as illustrations of architecture but as buildings with distinctive personalities.

I am aware that the selection will not go unchallenged. I can only say that it represents churches that have attracted me for a variety of reasons - intrinsic beauty, architectural distinction, historical significance, special features of interest or simply an indefinable appeal. In the process of choosing them I had to reject at least fifty others, sometimes on very utilitarian grounds. For example, it was surprising to find many interesting churches not only locked, which is understandable, but with no indication of where a key could be obtained. We should be grateful, therefore, to Parochial Church Councils who are still prepared to leave their churches open, and to the many people who take on the job of acting as key-holders when a church has to be locked. As a result it should be possible to obtain easy access to all the churches discussed in the book, and I hope the fact will inspire suitable donations from appreciative visitors.

Finally, it is a daunting thought that for every church chosen there is somebody who knows far more about it than I do. No doubt I shall soon get to hear of any errors, and I shall gratefully note corrections for future editions.

Lawrence Garner
Pant Glas, Oswestry.

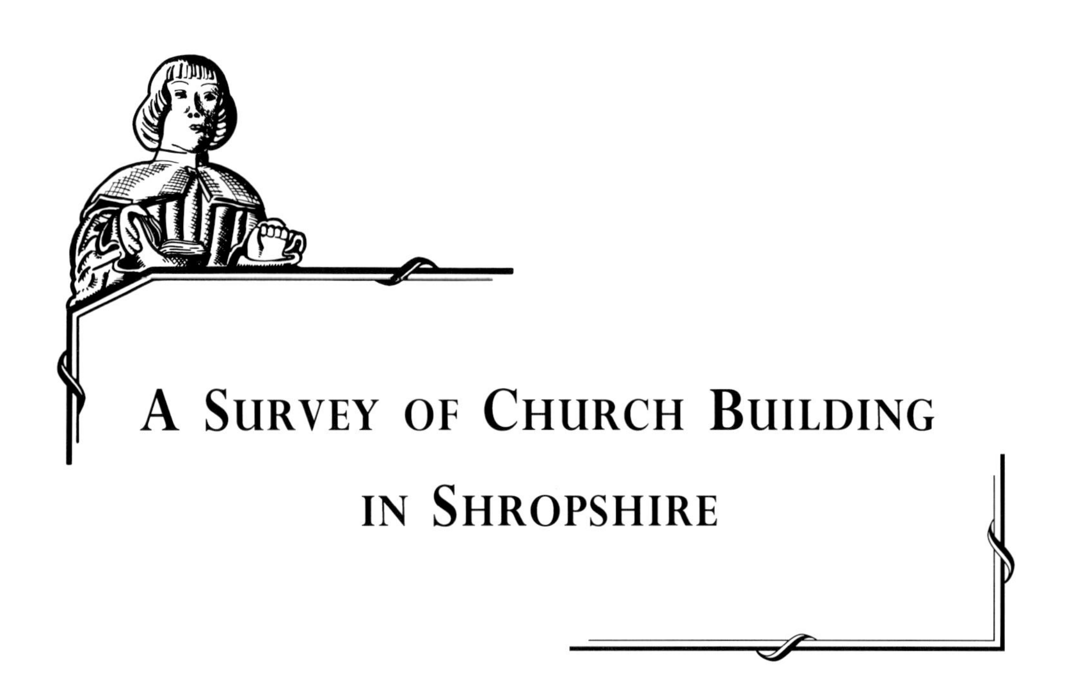

# A Survey of Church Building in Shropshire

Shropshire is fortunate in having churches that illustrate in their own fashion the whole progression of building styles from the eleventh century to the late flowering of the Victorian age. This introductory chapter is an attempt to pick a way through the complexities of ecclesiastical architecture and to show how national (and sometimes international) developments came to affect our familiar local churches.

The name 'Shropshire' is used throughout to denote the area of the modern county, so strictly speaking it is an anachronism when applied to events earlier than the sixteenth century. However, it seemed preferable to the repeated use of cumbersome expressions like "the area now known as Shropshire".

Church names in italics indicate that the building is one of those selected for more detailed discussion in the second half of the book.

# The Earliest Shropshire Churches

Thanks to a revival of interest in Celtic studies most people are now aware that Christianity in Britain did not begin with the arrival of Augustine's missionaries from Rome in 597. It took hold during the period of the Roman occupation, and following the departure of the Romans in the later years of the fourth century the faith was kept alive by Celtic churches in Scotland, Ireland and Wales. While Augustine's main concern was to convert the Saxon population he also had to try to reconcile his Roman Christian culture with the long-standing traditions of the Celtic Christians.

*An early Norman doorway at Stapleton church.*

Shropshire was, as always, caught between Welsh and English cultural developments. Strong Celtic influences remained during the post-Roman era and were never completely displaced by the encroachments of the Anglo-Saxons. Even after the construction of Offa's Dyke this part of the border continued to be a political and religious no-man's-land, and the fact was reflected in early ideas about church architecture.

The Celtic tradition had produced a 'single cell' church - a simple rectangle with no very marked division between nave and chancel - and evidence suggests that this may have been the model for most of the earliest Shropshire churches. (A former single-cell chapel has been traced within the church at *Barrow*, and no doubt there is similar evidence waiting to be discovered elsewhere in the county.)

Saxon Christianity favoured a more ambitious structure, and the typical church that emerged in Mercia during the ninth and tenth centuries was cruciform in shape, high in relation to its width and of 'twin-cell' design, with separate nave and chancel. The style can be traced today only in the church at *Stanton Lacy*, a notably wealthy area in late Saxon times, and it is likely that churches elsewhere were much less ambitious.

But this is speculation. The fact is that there are no surviving Saxon churches in Shropshire. Several have signs of Saxon origin, but other than at Stanton Lacy the traces are too slight to give a clue to the building's original appearance. During the phenomenal programme of church building following the Norman invasion most of Britain's earliest churches were demolished and replaced. In the whole of England only one of the wooden buildings of Saxon origin survived (in Essex) and the new churches were sturdily built in stone. However, existing stone churches in good repair were sometimes adapted, leaving earlier features.

Realistically, therefore, our study of church building has to start at quite a late date. As far as I am aware no surviving feature in any Shropshire parish church can be *proved* to be earlier than the eleventh century, by which time the style known as 'Romanesque' was well established and a plan consisting of a twin-cell structure with nave and chancel divided by an arch had become the norm.

The term 'Romanesque' is generally applied to the architecture of the late Saxon and early Norman period. As the name implies it was inherited from the Romans and persisted throughout western Europe until the late twelfth century. Without the advanced Roman technology, which included the use of concrete, the masons in the remoter regions

*Herringbone masonry, characteristic of the late Saxon and early Norman period.*

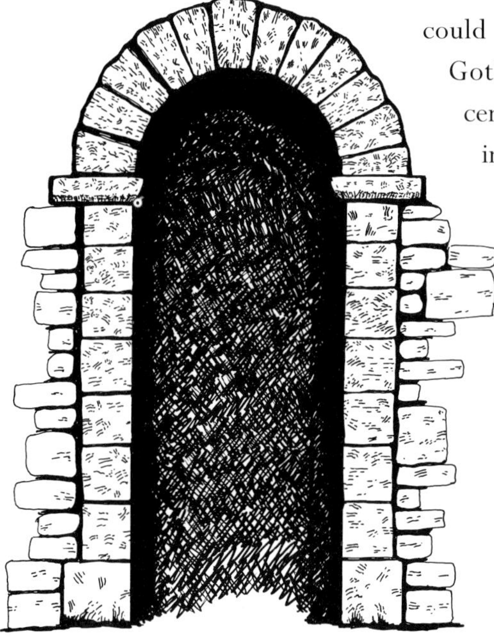

could produce only a crude and debased version of it, but until Gothic techniques became widely established in the thirteenth century, it was the only known way to construct a large building in stone.

The basic masonry techniques used in local Romanesque churches were either rubble construction with a rough attempt at coursing or the 'herringbone' method by which stones were laid on their edges, leaning to left and right in alternate courses. In either case the aim was to lock the stones in position under their own weight with no reliance on mortar. The resulting double-skinned walls would be several feet thick. Corners would be reinforced by primitive quoins or 'long and short work' - vertical blocks alternating with long stones that extended well into the masonry of the wall on each side. Timber roof trusses would be constructed to carry thatch.

*Above: A late Saxon doorway showing a simple Romanesque arch.*

*Below: A Norman window. The opening is set into the outside wall, with a splay towards the interior.*

The emphasis was on brute strength, so any supporting piers would be thick and circular (a circular column avoided corners that could form weak points). The most recognisable feature of Romanesque architecture, the semi-circular arch, was not only a piece of time-honoured design but also the accepted method of supporting heavy masonry above openings in walls that were too large for a single stone lintel. Slightly tapered stones called 'voussoirs' would be placed side by side to form a half-circle. When weight was applied on the arch the tapers prevented the stones from being forced out of place, but at the same time there was considerable lateral thrust, so a very heavy mass of wall was necessary on each side of an arch to hold it in place. Needless to say, Saxon and early Norman doorways and arches were invariably narrow.

Windows were tiny, partly to keep out the weather at a time when glass was unavailable and partly to avoid elaborate arch construction. Stout stones laid above a window could act as lintels, but since the windows were set in the middle of a thick wall their openings had to be widely splayed inside and out in order to admit as much light as possible. An example can be seen at *Barrow*. Norman windows were set on the outside of the wall so that only interior splaying was required.

*The north wall of Stanton Lacy church, showing Saxon pilaster strips and an early Romanesque doorway.*

These primitive techniques obviously provided little opportunity for grace or structural decoration. Any embellishment had to be superimposed afterwards and usually took the form of repetitive patterns carved within arches. Occasionally something more ambitious in the way of sculpture would be attempted, especially in the 'tympanum', the space between the top of a door and the arch above it. There are very early examples at Stottesdon and at Linley, where the carving takes the form of a pagan 'green man'. Externally the blank mass of towers and walls could be relieved by pilaster strips - thin, vertical lines of stone, remnants of which can be seen at *Stanton Lacy*.

## The Norman Influence

Romanesque building of this kind was general throughout northern Europe, so the Norman invasion did not produce major architectural changes in parish churches, and in most cases the builders would not have been required to adopt new methods. Until the establishment of the Norman monasteries in the mid-twelfth century there would have been little new architectural expertise available, so the late Saxon masons would have used their customary techniques even when working under a new regime.

But the Norman masons had greater experience of building in stone and more confidence in tackling ambitious structures. It is difficult to imagine local Saxon masons attempting a building on the scale of Shrewsbury Abbey or any of the monastic churches. The Normans also brought with them an artistic flair that resulted in richly-carved doorways of the kind that can be seen at *Heath, Holdgate, Edstaston* and several other churches.

*Heath Chapel, showing the pilaster buttresses and original windows on the west wall.*

Norman energy in the twelfth and early thirteenth centuries resulted in a very large number of new or adapted stone churches in Shropshire. Saxon parishes, served by clergy based at a principal church, could be very large indeed, so an early Norman development was the provision of small daughter chapels, of which *Heath* is a fine surviving example. It was only a matter of time before most of these acquired the status of parish churches, often undergoing considerable changes, one of the most common being the addition of a tower at the west end. This in turn would often entail the forming of a new doorway on the north or south side of the nave. The towers themselves were low and squat (*Clun* and *Holdgate* have typical examples), indicating a continuing caution in structural matters. A less ambitious alternative was a light bell-cote set on the west gable of the nave.

The flurry of Norman building activity included the expansion of small parish churches to accommodate a rising population. Where there was no tower the nave could be lengthened, but it was more common to expand sideways by creating aisles on one or both sides of the nave. This involved dismantling a side wall and replacing it with an arcade to support the roof. The extension would then take the form of a lean-to structure with a roof sloping down to a new low wall. Another method of gaining additional space was to add transepts - sideways extensions at the junction of nave and chancel, producing a cross-shaped or cruciform church. *Winstanstow* is an excellent early example of the method.

*The tympanum at Aston Eyre, portraying Christ's entry into Jerusalem.*

Alterations of this kind still embodied the Romanesque characteristic of massive strength, most visible in the piers of the arcades, but French influence is revealed in shapelier arches and more elaborate decoration. New chancel arches and doorways received particular attention. A basic form of embellishment was the cutting of the arch as a series of receding 'steps'. The steps could be continued down each side of the door or window, and decorated either with carved patterns or by making each step a raised moulding. Also common were 'shafts' - miniature attached columns in the jambs of doorways. Outstanding among many good surviving Norman doorways in Shropshire parish churches are those at *Edstaston* and *Holdgate*.

The piers supporting arcades also provided opportunities for embellishment. Their capitals - the points on which the arches rest - were normally decorated either with simple moulding or with carving, very often of foliage. But some of the finest Norman embellishment was reserved for the tympanum, the semi-circular area immediately above a door, which was often carved with sculptured figures in relief. The best Shropshire example is at *Aston Eyre*.

## The Gothic Revolution

The constraints of Romanesque architecture - bulky masonry, narrow arches and small windows - were eliminated by a single technological discovery that made possible the complexities of Gothic architecture.

We have seen that the Saxon and Norman builders equated mass with strength, and that wall openings and chancel arches were narrow and strongly supported on each side because semi-circular arches exerted a strong outward thrust. This was also the reason for the rarity of stone roofs during the Romanesque period - the thrust would have been directed laterally on to the walls, causing them to bulge out.

The breakthrough was the development of the pointed arch and the buttress. French masons of the early twelfth century discovered that putting weight on to a pointed arch produced a predominantly downward thrust, requiring much lighter support on each side to contain it. This was particularly important in the case of roofs and chancel arches because the thrust of a pointed arch against the outside walls could be easily contained by strategically-placed external buttresses. Stone roofs built on a framework of ribs now became possible since the walls only needed to be reinforced at the points where the ribs rested.

Timber roofing could be improved also. Hitherto the usual method of preventing the outward thrust of roof timbers had been to install heavy tie beams to hold the two sides of the roof together. Buttressing the principal rafters did away with the need for unsightly tie beams and allowed roofs to be opened up and beautified.

The pointed arch and the buttress were virtually the only basic constructional advances of the medieval period, but they made possible a wealth of artistic development, especially in window design. Since the walls between the buttresses now carried a greatly reduced load they could be made thinner, and larger window openings became possible, providing scope for tracery embellishment. From the late thirteenth century onwards church builders, freed from many of the old structural constraints, were able to strive for refinement and beauty.

In the 1820s Thomas Rickman produced his famous classification of English Gothic architecture, identifying three distinct stages - Early English (1170-1270),

*Battlefield church, erected between 1406 - 1409 incorporated windows in both the Decorated and Perpendicular styles.*

Decorated (1270-1370) and Perpendicular (1370-1500). These dates are, of course, extremely arbitrary. There was an appreciable time-lag before the successive Gothic styles arrived in Shropshire, and local masons continued to be cautious in adopting them. The county has a number of churches in which Norman and early Gothic styles were used together in a manner usually termed Transitional.

*Stepped lancet windows typical of the thirteenth century: they are unified by the hood-mould above.*

The two features that most often indicate an advance in fashion are the windows and the arcades. The early thirteenth century was the period of the lancet window - a tall, narrow, pointed opening, usually splayed on the interior side. There was still a reluctance to risk a single large opening, but the effect of a big window could be achieved by grouping lancets together. 'Stepped lancets' were a favourite arrangement in which a tall central window was flanked by others decreasing in height. The arrangement would be unified by a surrounding hood-mould.

Arcades changed in various ways. Sometimes the traditional circular piers were retained but the arches they supported were pointed. More often the piers themselves became more slender and elegant, perhaps taking an octagonal form or being decorated with pipe-like vertical mouldings. In more ambitious work the capitals of the arches would be embellished with stylised foliage ("stiff leaf") and it became usual to chamfer the edges of the arches. The 'steps' and the decorative carving found in so many Norman arches disappeared. New pointed chancel arches became more generous in size.

At High Ercall church the arcades, dating from about 1200, have Romanesque circular piers but the arches are tall and pointed with double chamfering. The chancel arch and tower arch are similar in style. St. Peter's, Rushbury, a church old enough to have herringbone masonry in its walls, acquired new interior features in about 1200, including an east window in the new fashion - three stepped lancets, embellished with shafts and capitals - and the chancel also has lancets in its other walls. Of the same period are the nave lancets and the south doorway, with waterleaf capitals on the shafts. At Shawbury the nave arcades have circular piers, but they are slender and have showy square capitals with carved embellishment. It is mainly of a scallop design but in two cases there is a pattern of foliage. The arches are still round-headed. The chancel arch, however, is moulded, chamfered and pointed in the new style.

These 'transitional' churches also include *Holy Trinity, Winstanstow*. It is a cruciform church of about 1200, where the transepts appear to have been built simultaneously, yet in the north transept the windows are of the usual Norman type - splayed and round-headed - while in the south transept they are pointed. The east windows are lancets and there is another early lancet over the blocked north door of the nave.

## EARLY ENGLISH INNOVATION

As the thirteenth century progressed cautious experiments gave way to the widespread adoption of full Gothic style. This was Rickman's 'Early English' period, when new opportunities for embellishment were eagerly seized. The new trend is seen most clearly in the design of windows, where 'plate tracery' made a first appearance. Typically it took the form of two or more lancet windows with an opening cut above them, sometimes a plain circle but more often a circle 'cusped' to form a trefoil or quatrefoil - a pattern of three or four leaves. The whole composition would be unified within a hood-mould. East windows became the subject of particular artistic attention.

*Plate tracery, an early method of embellishing windows by piercing the stonework above, in this case with a quatrefoil design.*

There is notable Early English work at Cleobury Mortimer, where the chancel arch is very tall and wide and elaborately moulded with three orders of shafts and stiff-leaf capitals. The

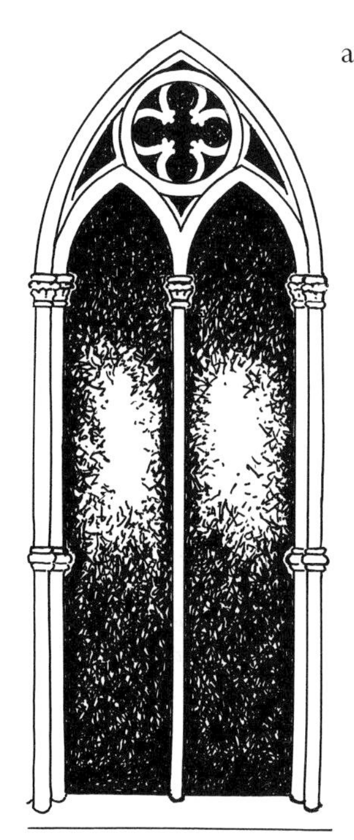

*A thirteenth century development of plate tracery: twin lancets and a quatrefoil incorporated into a single window.*

arcades are also typical thirteenth-century work, the south rather older, with round piers and chamfered arches. The east window has been restored but conforms to the Early English fashion for stepped lancets under a hood-mould. St. Andrew's, Shifnal, also shows some striking architectural advances. There is considerable Norman work at the east end of the church, but the nave and aisles are of the thirteenth century, revealed in the newly-fashionable octagonal piers and chamfered arches. The ambitious triple-chamfered tower arches date from the end of the century. However, the outstanding feature of the period here is the south porch, of two storeys and supported on the inside by vaulting - a feature rare in a Shropshire parish church in the mid-thirteenth century.

However, the two most complete Early English churches in Shropshire are at *Longnor* and *Acton Burnell*. Both built towards the end of the thirteenth century, they show how the new Gothic style could be used both plainly (at *Longnor*) and very ambitiously where enough money was available.

## The Decorated Period

The trend towards delicacy and adornment accelerated in the fourteenth century. Rickman's term 'Decorated' is particularly apt because it was a time of remarkable freedom of artistic expression. Buttresses were now widely adopted in order to lighten the walls and make much larger window spaces possible. These windows were no longer lancets but multiple lights, separated by mullions and surmounted by complex 'reticulated' tracery in flowing designs. Many were further beautified by the installation of stained glass, although very little now survives.

Arches and piers acquired genuine grace and the carving on the capitals became more complex and often more naturalistic. For the first time since the Norman period the mouldings of the arches themselves were decorated, often with the design known as 'ballflower'. Chancel arches, however, began to fall out of favour, to be replaced by wooden rood screens and lofts, which effectively cut off the chancel from the nave and provided ample opportunities for rich carving. The fashion for embellishment also extended to the exterior. The most striking new feature was the spire (not common in Shropshire), but minor elaborations included decorated pinnacles to towers and walls.

*Reticulated tracery of the fourteenth century: one of many curvilinear designs characteristic of the Decorated period.*

Shropshire has few fourteenth-century churches, perhaps because it was a lean time economically, but possibly because the wave of new building and enlargement in the previous two centuries had met the needs of the population. Decorated work is found largely in features added to existing churches and particularly in windows, although a great many new chancel screens must have been installed at this time and later destroyed by the Protestant reformers of the sixteenth century.

Much of *St. John the Baptist's, Hughley*, dates from this period, including some stained glass, some characteristic windows and a fine screen. Octagonal structures were common in the fourteenth century, but *Hodnet's* octagonal tower is unique in the county. The interior here is much restored, but the eastern end of the arcade is original, with its octagonal pier and chamfered arches. The east windows of the chancel, the south aisle and the Heber chapel are Victorian, but are designed to reproduce various Decorated styles of tracery.

Kynnersley church shows the transition from Early English to Decorated fashion in its chancel - the north and south windows are twin cusped lancets but the east window is a fine example of the new reticulated tracery. At *Ludlow* the hexagonal porch is a rarity, while the north aisle of about 1315 has a fine four-light west window with characteristic ballflower ornament (original on the outside). In the south chapel a Jesse window of this period has been greatly restored, but still contains original glass. There are further Decorated windows in the north transept.

St. Peter's, Worfield, is another church with much fourteenth-century remodelling, including the tower and spire, the octagonal arcades and some fine windows.

## Perpendicular - The Return to Formality

The end of the fourteenth century saw a reaction to the artistic freedom of the Decorated period and a return to severer and more disciplined architectural styling. The rectangle became a dominant motif. It can be seen in the towers of the time, which often feature stone panels, and also in a new kind of roof. The traditional pitched roof had survived for centuries because of the need to shed rain quickly, but the adoption of lead as a roof covering made possible a much lower pitch and led to a radical change in the external appearance of churches. Rain no longer dripped from overhanging eaves but ran into gutters at the bottom of the roof and was thrown off through spouts, which were often decorated by the fanciful carved heads called gargoyles. With no eaves in the way the walls of the tower, nave and chancel could be built up to form parapets - usually taking the form of battlements with pinnacles - which gave a unifying design to the whole building.

*The Perpendicular church at Ightfield shows the battlements, pinnacles and window tracery fashionable in the fifteenth century.*

The flatter roof obviously did away with the impressive show of roof timbers. They were replaced by boarding in a pattern of rectangular panels with bosses where the ribs intersected, providing scope for elaborate and colourful designs.

The effect of the Perpendicular style on church interiors can once again be seen most clearly in windows, where the free curves of the Decorated period were replaced by a pattern of mullions dividing rather flat-headed lights and incorporating a tracery of near-rectangular panels. The style can be seen most strikingly in the great west window of *Shrewsbury Abbey*.

*A Perpendicular window showing the fomal design typical of the fifteenth century.*

Carving in stone and wood continued to flourish. The rood screen was well-established, but there were further opportunities for carving in the 'parclose' screens separating chapels from the main body of the church. Arches, on the other hand, were rarely embellished, but gained impressively in height.

The imposing Perpendicular style was expensive and was often exploited as an ostentatious display of conspicuous wealth, whether personal or corporate. *Ludlow* parish church, greatly enlarged and remodelled in the fifteenth century, is a clear expression of commercial prosperity arising from the wool trade. *St. Bartholomew's* at Tong dates from the early part of the century and is the best Shropshire example of a wholly Perpendicular church, having been established as a collegiate foundation by the wealthy widow of the Lord of the Manor. Battlefield was another collegiate church, raised at the expense of Henry IV after the battle of Shrewsbury. Ordinary parish churches in Perpendicular style are harder to find (one stands in the small village of Ightfield) although there are examples of major rebuilding in the new style at Edgmond and Newport.

The most common Perpendicular addition to an older church was a tower, either brand new as at Cheswardine, Kinnerley and Loppington or as a rebuilding of the upper section of an older structure, as at *Holdgate*. The latter process can be seen in a great many churches with towers that are battlemented or pinnacled, and confirmation is often provided by a frieze immediately below the parapet. Elsewhere in Britain tall needle spires became common, but Shropshire has no spectacular examples (the most famous, at *St. Mary's, Shrewsbury*, belongs to the previous century).

Two exceptions to the general Gothic trend of the fifteenth century should be mentioned here. The church at *Melverley* and the chapel at Halston Hall, Whittington, were both built as timber-frame structures. They can be interpreted as low-cost buildings, but could equally represent the growing status of timber-framing in the latter part of the century. There are examples elsewhere of porches and belfries created in this way.

## The Barren Years

The years immediately following Henry VIII's break with Rome, which included the dissolution of the monasteries in the late 1530s, saw a notable expansion of domestic building and some dramatic changes in secular architecture, but the period was a stagnant one for church building.

One reason was that by 1540 every existing parish had a church, so the medieval surge of building and replacement came to an end. Another was the fact that the emergence of the Church of England led to a long period of confusion, when questions of theology and Church government took priority over mundane matters like building and maintaining churches. A third reason was the removal of monastic influence and authority, which had been a force behind the building of new churches.

A fourth reason was the final break-up of the feudal system and its replacement by a new breed of major landowners (often absentees) who were less inclined to accept responsibility for the creation or repair of parish churches, and did not regard that kind of philanthropy as a pious duty.

If few new churches were built many changes took place in existing ones - few of them for the better. Protestant zeal during the reign of Edward VI ensured that many symbols of 'Romanism' were eradicated. Medieval stone altars were replaced by communion tables, often with seating on three sides; rood lofts were dismantled, though occasionally the screens beneath them were retained; stained glass was broken up; colourful decorations such as wall paintings were covered; statues of saints were removed, leaving the empty niches which are frequently found in churches today.

*The bleak interior of Langley chapel.*

The *Langley Chapel* (a private venture) was the only new Shropshire church of the Elizabethan period, and its interior, surviving virtually intact, is a vivid reminder of the bleak legacy of the Protestant reformers.

The architectural stagnation continued into the first half of the seventeenth century, which was dominated by religious conflict culminating in the Civil War. It was not an atmosphere conducive to a close interest in church architecture, although Archbishop Laud restored some dignity by ordering the restoration of the altar to a fixed position at the east end within a railed sanctuary and backed by some form of reredos.

In Shropshire the few major rebuildings of the period, for example at *Benthall, Stokesay* and *Condover* were in an indeterminate style, although *Condover* gives us a clue as to what a new mid-seventeenth century church might have looked like. The nave is without aisles and therefore without the structural support of arcades. The wide span is made possible by a sophisticated hammer-beam roof (a similar but smaller roof was installed at *Benthall*) while the windows are straight-headed. These features indicate the beginnings of a departure from Gothic towards a style more akin to contemporary domestic architecture, a process that accelerated after the Restoration in 1660, when there was an upsurge of national interest in architecture, and particularly in classical forms derived from Italy.

## The Flowering of Classicism

Inigo Jones had pioneered the Palladian style of classical church building in the 1630s, but it was the influential work of Wren and his colleagues after the Great Fire of London that firmly established the new principles.

Wren's Italianate 'basilica' churches, resembling Roman temples, happened to suit the new Protestant ideas of worship. Late-medieval Gothic churches conformed in design to the Catholic precept that the Mass was a mystery not to be shared openly by the congregation, who came to hear the service but not to participate fully. Thus the chancel was emphatically divided from the nave, often by a screen. Post-Reformation worship laid more emphasis on preaching and encouraged full participation by a congregation who were entitled to see and hear everything.

The basilica churches were ideal for this purpose, being planned in an essentially theatrical way - as auditoria with the nave seating undivided from the sanctuary, which in effect became a stage giving the congregation a clear view of the altar. With the new emphasis on preaching the pulpit also acquired a dominant position. The ground plan was squarer, and in many churches this allowed for a gallery on three sides. Tall windows of clear glass brought a new lightness to the interior, which would be embellished by classical features such as columns, pilasters, painted ceilings and elaborate plasterwork. The classical idiom would be repeated on the entrance facade, which was often dominated by a columned porch or a giant portico.

The churches of Wren and his fellow architects have been termed 'Baroque'. The label implies an emphasis on elaborate decoration, and it is certainly true that their flamboyant style was far removed from the simple elegance of Inigo Jones and the Palladian architecture from which it derived.

*The classical interior of St. Alkmund's, Whitchurch - a startling innovation in 1712.*

The new fashion reached Shropshire in odd ways. In the 1670s *Bromfield* church - otherwise a mixture of medieval styles - acquired a strange painted ceiling over its chancel, and in 1689 the new church at *Minsterley* was built with a bizarre attempt at a classical facade. More widespread was a sudden distaste for rough medieval work. The urge to introduce classical elegance frequently resulted in fine roof timbers being plastered over and elaborate pulpits towering in ungainly fashion. Fortunately many of Shropshire's churches were remote and escaped drastic change. One innovation, however, was almost universal - the installation of box pews, often crammed in with little thought for aesthetic effect.

It was not until 1712 that the classical style really arrived in the county with the building of *St. Alkmund's, Whitchurch*. It was not a whole-hearted essay in classicism (its tower has Gothic echoes) but it was an architectural landmark, and was to remain so for many decades. Its elegant interior must have seemed revolutionary at the time.

*A contemporary engraving of the controversial new church of St. Chad, Shrewsbury.*

The torpor of the Church of England throughout most of the eighteenth century ensured that church building in Shropshire was desultory. New structures at Kinnerley, Montford, Cardeston and Longdon-on-Tern were unadventurous, and ecclesiastical architecture did not begin to match the sophisticated developments in Georgian domestic building until George Steuart (the architect of Attingham Hall) was invited to design a replacement for *St. Chad's, Shrewsbury* in the early 1790s. His new *St. Chad's*

was an innovative and highly individual classical structure with a circular nave that carried the notion of an auditorium to its logical conclusion. It is a church of national significance. Steuart was also responsible for the distinguished though less ambitious All Saints' at Wellington. At the same time the engineer Thomas Telford, with effortless versatility, was designing classical churches at *Bridgnorth* and Madeley.

This flowering of classicism produced splendid results but was short-lived. The grand style was essentially urban and did not transfer readily to the countryside. It was also expensive, of course, but rural conservatism would in any case have discouraged it. Nevertheless there are examples of the adoption of a homely classical style at *Frodesley* and in the abandoned church at Longford, near Newport. A few churches like Moreton Say and Great Bolas were given Georgian exteriors, and a great many received remodelled interiors incorporating galleries, box pews, new pulpits, tall windows and a plan abolishing the division between nave and sanctuary. *Longnor* is a good example.

Incidentally the new auditorium style proved ideal for nonconformist worship, and was adopted for most of the new wave of chapels built early in the nineteenth century.

## The Gothic Revival

The early years of the nineteenth century brought a more sustained enthusiasm for church building, inspired partly by the Evangelical revival following Wesley's breach with the Church of England. The formation of the Church Building Society in 1818 promoted an interest in the subject, while the Church Building Act soon afterwards provided funds administered by a Commission for the building of new churches where none existed, mainly in the new industrial towns and expanding city suburbs. *St. Luke's, Ironbridge*, was a 'Commissioners' church', and some of the principles involved are discussed in the section devoted to it later in the book.

This was a time of intense architectural controversy, and the thirties and forties saw a strong reaction in all branches of architecture against classicism and in favour of Gothic.

Ideas about church architecture came to be dominated quite disproportionately by two influences - the books written in the 1840s by the fanatical Gothicist A.W.N. Pugin and the propaganda of the Camden Society, a Cambridge University group dedicated to restoring medieval church architecture. Further pressure came from the devotees of the Oxford Movement, which urged a return to traditional Catholic practice in the Church of England, including an emphasis on the 'mystery of the Mass'.

This early Gothic revival was essentially ecclesiastical, motivated by a small group of specialist architects. During the same period important secular buildings in Shropshire towns were designed in the much-admired Greek Revival style, as was St. Catherine's, Whitchurch. Several country mansions were remodelled in the same fashion.

*Shrewsbury's new Roman Catholic cathedral of 1856 illustrates the results of the Gothic Revival.*

From the 1840s onwards, however, Victorian churches were built and restored almost exclusively in versions of Gothic, some of them highly individual. Theorists maintained that the fourteenth-century Decorated style represented the finest form of Christian architecture, although the thirteenth century was also admired (hence the proliferation of lancet windows in new churches and restorations of the mid-nineteenth century). The Perpendicular period was generally felt to have represented a debasement of

Gothic. But purism was short lived. From the 1850s onwards church architects felt free to indulge their whims in a variety of Gothic fancies.

The new churches were not, of course, exact copies of medieval structures, since they had to be adapted for Protestant worship. Indeed, several architects succeeded in getting the best of both worlds by combining a Gothic exterior with the spacious, open, well-lit interior associated with the classical churches. This had been done in the 1790s when Carline and Tilley rebuilt St. Alkmund's at Shrewsbury, and Commissioners' churches like *St. Luke's, Ironbridge* (1836) tended to follow the same pattern. Most village churches, however, were a compromise of the kind which we now accept as normal - a nave and chancel separated by a broad chancel arch that suggested a division without obstructing the congregation's view of the altar.

Many internal features which we now take for granted were introduced for the first time during this early wave of traditionalism. The robed choir occupying stalls in the chancel, for example, was a fashion that spread rapidly following an experiment by the Vicar of Leeds. Hitherto the accepted place for singers and musicians had been in the west gallery. Moving the choir often involved moving the organ too, and the appearance of many a church was ruined by the installation of a large and cumbersome instrument on one side of the chancel. The lectern, often in the form of an eagle, was another innovation of the early nineteenth century, as was the practice of raising the altar (and sometimes the chancel) on three steps.

## The Later Victorian Years

The story of Shropshire church architecture in the second half of the nineteenth century is not exciting, perhaps because the most spectacular work was being done in the large industrial towns of England. The few big churches of the period, like those at Coalbrookdale and Oakengates, are unremarkable, while small village churches were not seen as a challenge and were too often produced from an architectural assembly line.

Employing a nationally famous architect was no guarantee of getting an exceptional building. In fact the reverse was often true. Among the most illustrious Victorian ecclesiastical architects were Sir George Gilbert Scott, Sir Arthur Blomfield, Benjamin Ferry and G.E. Street. They all built churches in Shropshire, but if we examine the lists we can see very little distinguished work. Scott was responsible for churches at Welshampton and Donnington Wood, Blomfield designed churches at Jackfield, Glazeley and Neenton. Street was the architect at Withington, Church Aston, Waters Upton, Whixall, Lyneal and Oakengates (St. Matthew), while Ferry produced the churches at Fauls, Sambrook and Chetwynd. They are all safe, competent Gothic jobs, but it is hardly a roll of honour.

The reason is that commissioning a small village church from a famous practitioner was really like ordering a product from a factory - it was likely that the drawings would be produced in 'house style' by one of an army of assistants and given only a cursory nod by the master, who would concentrate on commissions involving greater prestige.

It was probably better value for money to engage a competent local architect who could run up a church from books of standard drawings. The Shrewsbury architect Edward Haycock, for example, was a prolific builder in the 1840s. Having made his mark with some notable essays in the Greek Revival fashion (including Millichope Hall, the Royal Salop Infirmary and Shrewsbury's Music Hall) he adapted quite effortlessly to Gothic and produced a string of churches at Newcastle, Middleton-in Chirbury, Chapel Lawn, Dorrington, Cressage, Cruckton and Hope. His son was responsible for Christ Church, Shelton, St. Andrew's, Welsh Frankton and Holy Trinity, Weston Lullingfields.

Another Shrewsbury architect much in demand in the fifties and sixties was S. Pountney Smith, who built at Harley, Leaton, Uffington, Hope Bowdler, Preston Gubbals and Shrewsbury (St. Giles). Two urban churches (*St. Luke's, Ironbridge* and

Christ Church, Wellington) were contributed by Thomas Smith of Madeley. Members of the Penson family practised in Wrexham and Oswestry, undertaking a mixed bag of commissions that included Holy Trinity, Oswestry and St. Agatha's, Llanymynech. W.H. Spaull of Oswestry built the first version of the little church at Rhydycroesau and also the remarkably inventive *Christ Church* for the Congregationalists of Oswestry. Occasionally we find the work of a local amateur, two notable examples being St. Barnabas, Hengoed (now demolished) by the Revd. A. R. Lloyd, and the highly individual *St. Michael's, Llanyblodwel*, the creation of its incumbent, the Revd. John Parker.

These lists are by no means exhaustive. The county acquired many other new Victorian churches, and when we take into account the wave of restorations in the last quarter of the century the total picture of ecclesiastical building work is astonishing. The activity tailed off in the 1890s, but the turn of the century saw at last some departures from standard Gothic, including new churches at Peplow and *Richards Castle* by Richard Norman Shaw, one of the outstanding late Victorian architects, and the novel half-timbered structure at Little Stretton.

*The unusual bullet-shaped tower and spire of Llanyblodwel church.*

A word needs to be said about Victorian restoration, a practice that has been more reviled than applauded. The term 'restoration' is a little misleading. It can refer to remedial work to rectify dilapidation (there is no doubt that by the end of the nineteenth century the majority of Shropshire's older churches were suffering from some degree of neglect) and we should appreciate the fact that so many churches were saved. It can also refer to more dubious practices.

In an age of increasing population with church attendance as the norm many small churches had to be enlarged, and this could lead to drastic alteration of the original fabric. Worse still were the cases where alterations resulted from a distaste for the untidy accretions of the centuries and a desire to conform to fashion. It has to be said that this attitude was not confined to the Victorians; in the fifteenth century it was common to add embellishments to older churches - new porches were added with little regard for clashing styles, towers received new tops, roofs were adorned with battlements and finials. In the eighteenth century stone churches were encased in brick and roof timbers hidden behind plaster ceilings. In spite of today's strict controls it is not uncommon to see incongruous modern 'improvements' in churches - at *Alberbury*, for example, a particularly fine medieval arcade has been filled in with plate glass.

Most of the faults of Victorian restoration arose from the deep-seated belief that Gothic was the only authentic ecclesiastical style. The unfortunate results of this aesthetic blindness can be seen vividly at *Frodeseley*, a tiny classical church which was enlarged in 1859 by adding a lean-to north aisle in a different, more uniform stone and a totally alien style. The same thing happened at *Benthall*, where a Gothic vestry was added to a seventeenth-century building.

In a church which was the result of successive waves of medieval building there could be a problem in deciding the most appropriate style for renewals or additions. While many such projects were worked out in seemly if uninspiring fashion (for example the new chancel at *Condover*) the decisions could sometimes be perverse. It can only have been through unimaginative pedantry that *Alberbury*, a big church crying out for a majestic east window, was given a new east end consisting of a monumental blank wall pierced by mean neo-Norman lancets.

The eighteenth-century taste for plaster has already been mentioned. Victorian restorers usually scraped this off on the grounds that it was not authentic. Sometimes the results could be beneficial in revealing interesting hidden features such as the wall paintings at *Claverley*, the hammer-beam roof at Shifnal or the fine carved barrel roof at Selattyn, but more often the end result of scraping walls was a smoothed-out baring of the original stonework that is far from appealing. *Holy Trinity, Wistanstow* is a striking example.

Many other instances of the philistine approach can be see in Shropshire churches, but they are balanced by work that shows great sympathy with the spirit of a building. J.L. Pearson's restrained design for the east end of *Shrewsbury Abbey* is a masterpiece, and most architects seem to have been sensitive in cases of genuine historical significance. The county's important Norman churches, for example, emerged remarkably intact.

The biggest regret must be that so many restorations produced an overall blandness in place of the haphazard variety that must have existed in so many medieval churches. But that is a late twentieth-century view, and quite likely to be reversed by future generations.

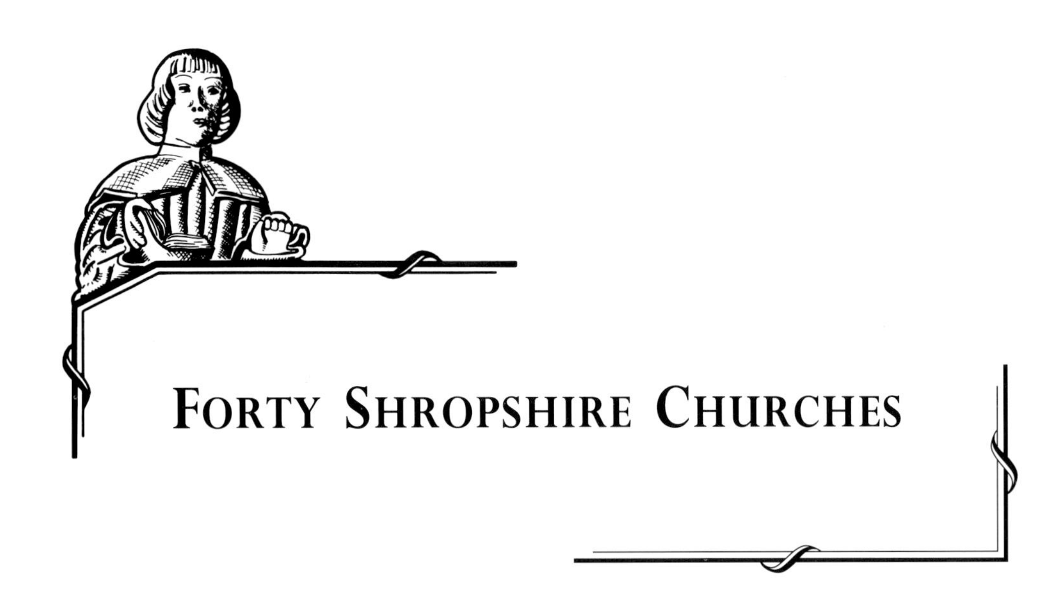

# FORTY SHROPSHIRE CHURCHES

These commentaries on selected churches are presented in alphabetical order by town or village. The churches are located by means of Ordnance Survey grid references (Landranger map series) and each reference is preceded by its sheet number. Shropshire is virtually covered by sheets 126, 127, 137 and 138, although Whitchurch is isolated on sheet 118.

# ACTON BURNELL (ST. MARY)

*126: 534019*
*7 miles south-east of Shrewsbury.*

It is easy to miss the church at Acton Burnell. Invisible from the modern village streets, it is found in a secluded spot between the ancillary buildings of the Hall (now Concord College) and the remains of Richard Burnell's fortified manor house.

From the architectural point of view it is one of Shropshire's most important churches. Despite renewal and some additions it remains the county's outstanding thirteenth-century structure - and a particularly rich one because Richard Burnell could afford the best.

He was secretary and chaplain to the future Edward I, and when his patron came to the throne in 1272 he continued to enjoy royal favour, becoming Lord Chancellor and Bishop of Bath and Wells. In the early 1280s Burnell decided to build a new house to replace the Shropshire family home, and was granted a royal licence to 'crenellate' - in other words to build a castle. As it turned out the crenellation was nothing more than a status symbol, and the 'castle' was intended as a comfortable residence.

The substantial ruins, with the distinctive semi-detached corner towers, stand next to the church, which was also built at Burnell's expense. Its precise date is unknown, though it probably preceded the new house. Although cruciform in plan it does not seem to have had the usual central tower, and the present small tower was slipped in rather apologetically in the nineteenth century.

A preliminary walk around the outside shows that the builder could afford something more than the functional church normally found in a remote village. The entrance porch on the north side has an enriched recess designed for a carved figure. The eaves of the north wall are embellished by corbels with grotesque heads, while the buttresses on the west front have multiple run-offs towards the bottom. The east window is particularly elaborate, with two pairs of twin lancets, each with a trefoil circle above and the whole group surmounted by a big cinquefoil. The lancet window was one of the basic features of thirteenth-century (Early English) architecture and there are single examples in the nave, but in the side walls of the chancel a rich effect was achieved by grouping lancets together and unifying them by a single run of carving in their heads.

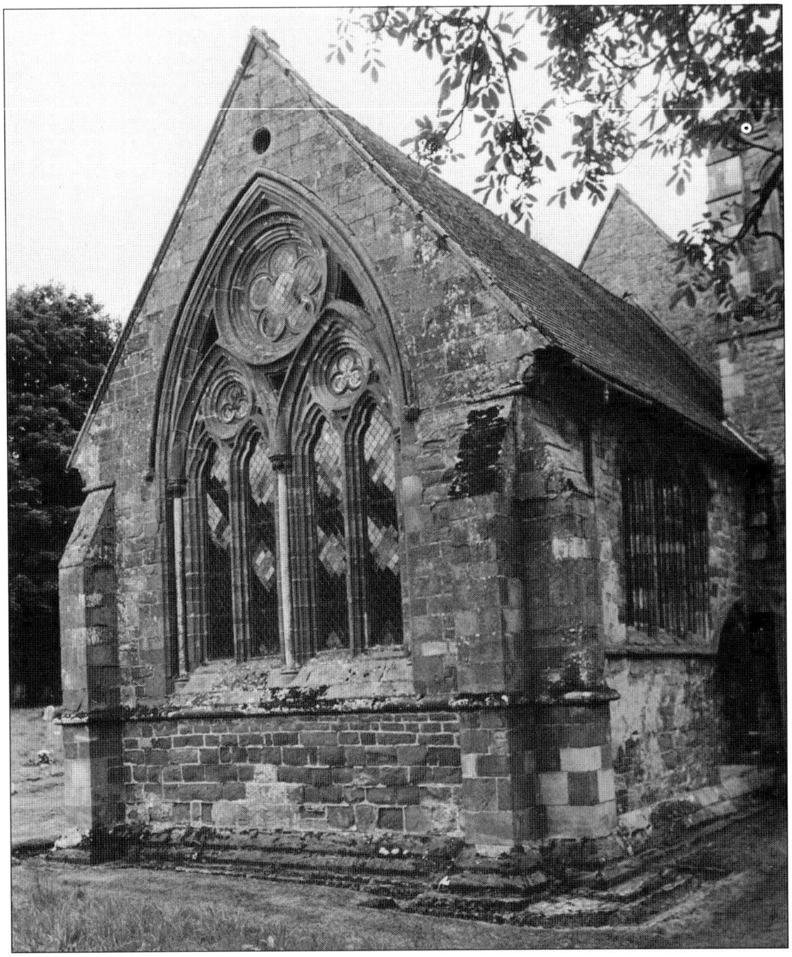

*Acton Burnell Church, showing the eleborate 13th century east window.*

There is no immediate sense of wealth on stepping into the church. The nave is distinctly austere, with the main light coming from the large west window with its three stepped lancets, but one would not expect elaboration in a part of the church that fulfilled in the middle ages many of the functions of a church hall. It is at the east end that expensive craftsmanship becomes evident.

Look first at the chancel and transept arches. There is nothing skimped about them; they have heavy multiple moulding and rest on a complex arrangement of short shafts with decorated capitals (some with stiff-leaf carving) and bases that feature foliage or modelled heads. In the sanctuary the piscina is on the grand scale, with its own miniature shafts and capitals. The enrichment of the chancel side windows, already noted on the exterior, is repeated inside, with the addition of Purbeck marble shafts between the lights.

The small hole on the north side of the chancel has been explained as a means by which a hermit could participate in the Mass from an external cell, but it is perhaps more likely to have been a 'lepers' squint' for the benefit of parishioners with infectious diseases.

Every feature noted so far has been typical of the late thirteenth century. In the transepts the work of later generations begins to intrude. The tomb recess in the south transept, with its ogee arch, belongs to the fourteenth century, while the north transept contains an array of monumental art of the same, and later, periods. In the north-east corner is a tomb chest with crocket decoration and a fine brass of Sir Nicholas Burnell, who died in 1382. On the East side is a gigantic, almost architectural, monument to Sir Richard Lee (died 1591). He and his wife lie in effigy, with their nine daughters carved rather perfunctorily in a neat row behind them, while their three sons occupy more privileged places at their father's head and feet. On the opposite wall is a familiar form of Jacobean memorial, showing husband and wife kneeling to face each other across prayer desks. In other examples of this kind (for example at Condover) inferior workmanship could result in figures of unattractive dumpiness, but here the carving is of high quality - in fact it is the work of Nicholas Stone, sculptor to Charles I. Again the children are shown, this time in ascending order. The memorial, of about 1632, is to Sir Humphrey Lee. Later monuments in the transept commemorate members of the Smythe family and are on a more modest scale. The floor, incidentally, retains its medieval tiles, some with their designs strikingly preserved.

Before leaving the church it is worth examining the octagonal font, which is again of the thirteenth century and features shafts and arches on each face.

# ALBERBURY (ST. MICHAEL AND ALL ANGELS)

*126: 358144*
*10 miles west of Shrewsbury on B4393.*

Modern Alberbury is an ill-defined sort of village lying beside the B4393 due west of Shrewsbury, but in the early middle ages its castle and priory made it a place of some consequence. The sketchy ruins of the castle still stand and there are residual remains of the priory some distance away, but the dominant building today is the church of St. Michael and All Angels.

*Alberbury Church: the south chapel.*

It stands on a rise in the old village centre, and the view from the outside is of an odd assembly of components, the strangest being the fortress-like tower with its rare pitched roof. Its lancet windows are typical of its late thirteenth-century date. (Like many church towers on the troubled border it was no doubt required to double as a refuge from time to time.) It is possible also to pick out the nave, the chancel with a slightly lower roof line and the tall south chapel.

This chapel conceals the real size of the church as you approach the south door, so that the length of nave and chancel comes as a surprise. The other immediate impression is one of darkness, caused partly by an inexplicable decision in the 1840s to rebuild the chancel in a version of Norman style. As a result the near-blank east chancel wall has two small round-headed windows and a circular one above, all coloured and admitting the minimum of light. To right and left are lurid lancets.

However, it is unnecessary to venture into the chancel to see the most striking features of the church. The late thirteenth-century nave is noted for its fine roof - the arched braces form full semi-circles and there is a lavish display of wind braces, which had the functional purpose of preventing lateral distortion of the roof timbers but which could also be exploited, as here, for decorative effect. There are no fewer than five rows of them on each side, formed into quatrefoil patterns.

The centre of interest, however, is the south chapel, now known as the Loton Chapel. The first buildings at nearby Loton Park were erected for the Leighton family in the seventeenth century, and the chapel is a repository of Leighton monuments. It dates from the fourteenth century and has an imaginative window of that period, with tracery based on the design known as the 'spheric triangle', resembling a casually-sketched leaf. At the turn of the century the window was glazed as a memorial to the third Sir Baldwyn Leighton. The artist was his daughter Barbara, who had apparently been much influenced by Burne-Jones, and she produced a pleasing example of Art Nouveau - a pair of kneeling angels beneath a design of roses.

The east wall of the chapel once had a huge window, its outline still visible on the outside. Now the wall bears monuments, and they repay inspection. Over the altar is a finely-wrought plaque to Dorothy Leighton who died in 1688, and to one side are tablets commemorating Bryan Leighton, a pioneer of aviation, and his son John. Both died in the service of the Royal Flying Corps. The panelling in the lower west wall contains other memorials fashioned unusually out of thin sheet metal.

As a contrast to these restrained tributes it is worth studying the two Lyster memorials in the nave. Sculpted in the worst eighteenth-century taste, they both feature ungainly *putti* or cherubs, one of them weeping unconvincingly. Finally, since unkind remarks have been made about some of the Alberbury glass, it is only fair to draw attention to the inconspicuous window to the west of the doorway. It glows with browns, golds and greens and has been executed with restraint and artistry.

## ATCHAM (ST. EATA)

*126: 542092*
*3 miles south-east of Shrewsbury on B4380.*

Since the re-routing of the A5 which used to run straight through the village, Atcham has become a much more tranquil settlement. If you turn into the road to Cross Houses on the Shrewsbury side of the river and park in the space immediately on your left you have the bonus of strolling peacefully across John Gwynne's elegant bridge, built in 1770 and now a footpath.

St. Eata's church is idyllically placed right on the river bank. Built in roughly-coursed sandstone blocks of irregular sizes, it has a tower which begins as Norman and ends as Perpendicular, illustrating the very common fifteenth-century practice of re-topping old towers with something more elegant - in this case a parapet with gargoyles and a frieze below. Its lower part is said to contain stones 'rescued' from the Roman ruins at nearby Wroxeter. Very noticeable on the north and south walls of the church are crude buttresses dated 1817 and no doubt built hurriedly to prevent a threatened collapse.

The late-Norman west door is particularly fine, flanked by five orders of bold shafts, though the present door is on the south side, and on entering you could be forgiven for thinking that collapse is imminent. The door hangs at an angle and the roof timbers over the chancel have a distinct list. The walls lean alarmingly - or so it appears. In fact they are 'battered', a perfectly sound technique of founding a wall on a very broad base and tapering it to the top. Obviously it was not considered dangerous by the restorers, who scraped the walls but otherwise did a restrained job and mercifully avoided forcing St. Eata's into a bland neo-Gothic mould.

It was a wise step to remove the west gallery, leaving exposed the impressive tower arch that soars to a height that would only have been contemplated during

*Atcham Church.*

the Perpendicular period. (Unless, of course, the arch is Victorian - the darkness makes close study difficult.) The problem of re-siting the organ was solved, uniquely perhaps, by placing it on the floor at the west end and letting it extend through the tower arch.

As you turn to the nave your attention is caught by the distinctive stained glass of the large north window; it is a memorial to Blanche Parry, "*Chief gentlewoman of Queen Elizabeth's privy chamber, whom she faithfully served from her Highness' birth, dying at court the 12th of February 1589 aged 82. Entombed at Westminster, her bowels at Bacton in the County of Hereford.*" There is a small picture of Blanche with the Queen. Bacton church, from which the window was transferred, contains a more famous monument to this lady who endured so long in a notoriously tough job. The small north window nearby is of very early date. The church's dedication to a seventh-century saint makes it certain that the present thirteenth-century structure was a replacement, and the incorporation of this window is added evidence. Its rare triangular head could identify it as late Saxon.

The chancel screen seems out of keeping with the rest of the church. Its gilded embellishments have a late eighteenth-century look and would go well with a three-decker pulpit. Is this something that survived the restorers in spite of the need to fit a remarkably extensive range of new choirstalls around it? Before entering the chancel it is worth studying the priest's desk, which is richly embellished with carvings portraying the parable of the Prodigal Son. They have been tentatively claimed as the work of the early sixteenth-century artist Durer, who worked in Nuremburg and produced some notable church carving. Whether or not they are the work of the master they clearly belong to that European tradition and have much in common with the more modern Oberammagau carvings on the reredos at Tong.

For some English work of roughly the same period look on the wall immediately opposite. The incised slab commemorating Edward Burton and his wife (brought from old St. Chad's, Shrewsbury, following its collapse) is a naive piece of work with a homely charm seldom found in this kind of memorial. Seven daughters are ranged below the couple.

Early stained glass is so rare in Shropshire that we must be grateful for the late-medieval east window, even though it is another Parry memorial brought from Bacton. Miles Parry's family kneels below three large standing figures, exquisitely portrayed in pale greys, browns and golds - a reproach to the lurid taste of so many Victorian practitioners. There are many good reasons for visiting St. Eata's but this is certainly the best.

## BARROW (ST. GILES)

*138: 657998*
*2½ miles east of Much Wenlock off B4376.*
*(The church is usually locked, but the key can be obtained from the house opposite).*

At first sight there is nothing remarkable about St. Giles'. It stands away from the road, sharing a drive with Barrow Hall and forming part of a group that includes the village school and a low range of early nineteenth-century almshouses. Its plain Norman tower has been given a pyramid roof and its rubble stonework has been neatly pointed.

If you walk round to its little chancel, however, you will see the irregular blocks of masonry that make up the earliest part of the building, while the double-splayed window on the north side is evidence of Saxon origins. It has been reliably established that the present chancel was an eleventh-century rebuild (probably to about the same size) of an earlier chapel established by Wenlock Priory. This makes it one of the most important pieces of late Saxon work to have survived in the county.

Standing within the chancel, which is less than twelve feet wide, you get a vivid impression of the tiny proportions of the earliest churches. It is divided from the

*Barrow Church. The tower door in the foreground, with a decorated tympanum, was the original west doorway to the church.*

nave by a flattened Saxon arch of simple construction with an emphatic hood-mould and no decoration, and on the south side is a doorway in similar style - puzzling because it has been crudely inserted by cutting into a window space. This window is of the single-splayed Norman type, so it cannot be much older than the doorway. In the north wall is the double-splayed window previously mentioned, while the east and south windows date from the 1850s.

The nave is early Norman and still has two small single-splayed windows, but the interesting feature here is the west doorway - tall and narrow with a tympanum that is naively carved on the tower side. It was evidently the original entrance, left in place when the twelfth-century tower was built. At some point the church was enlarged by the addition of a north transept, though there appears to be some doubt about when it first happened. The present structure dates from the late seventeenth century and provided wall space for a rash of monuments, but it appears to have been virtually rebuilt in the Victorian period.

A big hatchment on the north wall is a reminder of the influence of the local Forester family; in fact a mid-Victorian Lord Forester was responsible for the attractive window in the south wall. Its two lights commemorate in charming fashion a nurse and a housekeeper. A little further to the west is a brass plaque in memory of Charlie Rowe, another long-serving member of the Forester staff.

## BENTHALL (ST. BARTHOLOMEW)

*127: 657025*
*3 miles north-east of Much Wenlock off B4375.*

St. Bartholomew's church lies in the shadow of Benthall Hall, the Elizabethan mansion owned by the National Trust and open to the public. In fact it is easy at first glance to mistake the church for an outbuilding because its appearance is distinctly un-churchlike.

The nave and chancel of 1667 (built after the original church had been severely damaged in a Civil War skirmish) have received various additions, and as you approach through the gate from the south it is possible to see the components of the building. In 1887 a lean-to vestry in grey stone was added to the east end, and it can be seen projecting rather awkwardly, built in a determinedly Gothic style that fails to match the original church.

At the west end the most obvious feature is a tall square tower with an arch at ground level, a sundial above and a window at the top. The arch was once the entrance, though the door is now blocked up and contains a seat. A small timber-framed belfry is set above the original west wall. In 1893 it was decided to provide

*The south side of Benthall church, showing the effect of piecemeal alterations.*

a roomier entrance and a more convenient staircase to the gallery, so a brick extension was added, with an apse-like feature containing the stairs. At the same time the miniature tower was constructed and the sundial, embellished with a mosaic representation of an eye, was installed.

Amid all the changes the old door was rescued, and you now go through it to enter a church which at first seems entirely of the eighteenth century, with box pews, an exquisite miniature organ and a pulpit and reader's desk flanking the chancel arch. But closer inspection reveals details of its 1667 origin. The chancel arch, for example is a wide flattened curve that has no Gothic pedigree, the nave windows are plain and segment-headed while the roof is a hammer-beam structure half-hidden by plaster. It is a fair guess that the plaster was a piece of eighteenth-century tidying up. There were further modifications in 1892 when the three-decker pulpit was dismantled and the materials recycled to produce the present pulpit and desk. No doubt the change meant less neck-craning for the congregation, but it is a pity to have lost a feature that hardly survives in Shropshire now.

A more acceptable change was the removal in the 1970s of the two big gentry pews that used to stand in the chancel. They were obtrusive in this tiny building, and the clear space restores the proportions of the interior. The east window is something of a disaster - Victorian stepped lancets in the best thirteenth-century style, probably contemporary with the new vestry and just as incongruous.

We can be thankful that when the chancel was 'restored' the finest monument was retained. It is mounted on the north wall of the sanctuary and is a magnificent thing, the tablet framed sumptuously in gold and surmounted by an open pediment with a coat of arms. It commemorates Ralph Brown (died 1709) and his wife, who was a Benthall. The huge and startling painting on the chancel wall arouses mixed feelings. Dating from 1952, it is Edward Burra's portrayal of the Coronation of the Virgin. Mary is being crowned rather inconspicuously in the top left-hand corner while most of the picture swirls with a string of exuberant, frightened and puzzled figures, including a frenzied band of musicians. Slightly tongue-in-cheek, it is a compelling picture, but one that really belongs in a spacious gallery.

It bids the visitor a noisy farewell to this most peaceful of churches.

## BRIDGNORTH (ST. MARY MAGDELENE)

When Thomas Telford was called in to design a new church on the site of Bridgnorth's old castle chapel he was left in no doubt about his priorities. What was needed was a fitting structure to close off East Castle Street, the town's smartest thoroughfare, and the need for the facade to face the street meant that the alignment was north-south instead of the customary east-west.

The church, begun in 1792, is certainly impressive and very much in the restrained classical style favoured by Telford. The facade is unified by a full-width pediment supported by round and square attached columns. The tower rises above it in three stages - a square base of rusticated stone, a smaller square belfry with attached columns, and a final polygonal drum surmounted by a dome.

A preliminary walk around the church will show the simplicity of Telford's design. It was originally a plain rectangle with immensely tall round-headed windows and a recurring pattern of twin pilasters. In 1876 the celebrated architect Sir Arthur Blomfield was commissioned to build an apse to accommodate the sanctuary and allow room for an organ and vestry. He was careful to blend his own work with Telford's in seamless fashion - on the outside, at least.

A first glance inside will show the unfortunate effect of the apse on the interior. Telford's plan followed quite closely that of a Roman basilica, and provided for a sanctuary in a shallow recess and two rows of giant columns to create a nave and side aisles. The apse, embellished with stained glass, no doubt added Gothic mystery but was totally out of keeping with a concept that relied on clear light flooding the interior through those huge windows.

Fortunately the nave windows escaped coloured glass, so the first impression is still one of light and space, greatly enhanced by the removal of the former side galleries. The Ionic columns have enormous impact, rising from massive square bases and not pretending to be anything but a structural necessity. The flat ceiling adds to the sense of a building reduced to its basic essentials and acquiring great dignity thereby. In fact it is an engineer's building, and Blomfield's attempt to continue the classical theme with round-headed windows and small pilasters seems fussy by contrast.

There is little point in walking round in search of small details because they are not there. It is enough to sit at the back and admire Telford's achievement in designing a building of modest size and giving it genuine grandeur.

*This old engraving of St. Mary's church, Bridgnorth, shows Telford's original east end before the addition of an apse in 1876.*

## BROMFIELD (ST. MARY)

*137: 482768*
*3 miles north-west of Ludlow on A49.*

Bromfield is a village split in two by the wide sweep of the A49, and it it easy to speed through it without being aware of its attractions. As the former estate village of Oakly Park it has its share of Victorian features like the charming school, the big rectory and attractive cottages, but several centuries before that it was the site of an important priory.

The priory gatehouse remains, very picturesque with its stone ground floor and timber-framed upper storey over a wide arch, but nothing survives of the monastic foundation except the nucleus of the church. As you approach it from the gate-

*Bromfield church.*

house it has a square and stumpy look, the result of the loss of its chancel and the later addition of a wide north aisle. This aisle and the tower date from the thirteenth century.

Like many other monastic foundations Bromfield was sold to a private owner at the Dissolution, and if you walk round to the south side you can see the one surviving wall of the Elizabethan house Charles Foxe built after demolishing the chancel. He incorporated into it the south transept, the tower and the space beneath, but in 1658 the church was restored to use, with the tower area reclaimed as the chancel.

All this can be clearly detected if you pass through the impressive porch and make straight for the chancel. Behind the altar is the blocked chancel arch of the monastic church. To the left is the restored arch to the former north transept, while the corresponding south transept arch has disappeared completely and been replaced by a new wall.

But this is not what visitors come to Bromfield to see. The church's unique attraction is overhead - a remarkable painted roof executed in naive fashion by Thomas Francis in 1672. The original scheme covered the chancel walls as well and was the dubious benefaction of Richard Herbert of Oakly Park. If he was hoping for something along the lines of the Sistine Chapel he must have been disappointed, because the result was a random representation of stocky and rather ugly cherubs entwined in lengthy texts and surrounded by grey clouds. The centrepiece is a representation of the Trinity. Ecclesiastical art of a different kind appears in the large triptych over the altar, dignified Victorian work by Charles Buckeridge who specialised in church fittings of this kind (there is another example in the church at *Richards Castle*). The assemblage rests on a gilded reredos and is surmounted by a splendid red and gold canopy.

Returning to the north aisle we find lancet windows of the thirteenth century, although the aisle east window is in the later Decorated style. They are now filled with stained glass in the restrained and careful style of C.E.Kempe, one of the foremost Victorian artists in this medium. His delicate glass in the west window does much to relieve the austerity of the nave, which must have been even more severe when its eighteenth-century plaster ceiling was in place. One great virtue of the much-maligned Victorian restorers was that they almost invariably ripped out these ceilings, and at Bromfield the operation revealed a particularly fine series of roof timbers from the Elizabethan age.

## CHIRBURY (ST.MICHAEL)

*137: 262985*
*3 miles north-east of Montgomery on A490.*

St. Michael's is an unusually large church for a small, scattered village, and it has an imposing presence on its roadside site, with the venerable Herbert Arms at its gates and the timber-framed village school behind it.

Its size is explained by the fact that the nave is a survival of a monastic church built when a community of Augustinian Canons was transferred here from nearby Snead. Strictly speaking the Canons were not monks but priests who took similar vows and emulated the monastic life without being enclosed. Their original church was no doubt constructed to the usual monastic pattern, with a nave, transepts and an elaborate chancel. The base of the massive tower appears to date from the early fourteenth century, but the decorative top section has all the signs of a fifteenth-century adaptation. At some stage the chancel and transepts were demolished, leaving the spacious nave, to which a new brick sanctuary was rather oddly tacked on in 1733

The big west door opens into a very dark tower space (there is a light switch inside on your right). It is worth pausing to look at the elaborate wall monument to John Pritchard (died 1728), a tablet flanked by Corinthian columns and surmounted by a wavy pediment with a coat of arms. It is a naive piece of work -

*Chirbury church. The decorative top to the tower is an unusually elaborate Perpendicular embellishment to the earlier structure.*

an attempt by a local craftsman to meet the demands of the new classical fashion in memorials.

The exterior of the church does not prepare you for the sheer size of the nave, an effect emphasised by the fact that the north and south aisles are too narrow to detract from the central space. The sense of height, too, is enhanced by fairly light fifteenth-century roof timbering and what would be a clerestory if it had windows. The impressive arcades, leaning in a manner reminiscent of St. David's Cathedral, are in the Transitional style of the early twelfth century, with big, plain circular piers supporting pointed chamfered arches. All the nave windows are Victorian, designed in Early English style with twin lancets surmounted by a circular light - a device known as plate tracery.

From the scale of the nave it is possible to visualise the effect of the original church, with a chancel doubling its present length. The restorers in the 1870s reinforced the scale by building a huge arch for a chancel that is now quite short. You enter it by way of steps flanked by rather self-important curled brass rails, with a fine eighteenth-century chandelier overhead. The triple-lancet east window contains some intricate Victorian glass, but the interesting windows are those to north and south, which are executed with some delicacy and in a style and colouring associated with the Pre-Raphaelites.

There is further stained glass in the south aisle, where the chapel is lit by an

*Claverley church. The battlements, finials and other decorative work of the fifteenth century conceal a much earlier interior.*

attractive Annunciation. The two adjacent windows appear to be typically Victorian in design, but in fact the western one belongs to the 1930s and shows an astonishing conservatism.

## Claverley (All Saints)

*138: 793934*
*5 miles east of Bridgnorth.*

Approached by minor roads and narrow lanes, Claverley is now well off the beaten track, but it must have been a place of some importance until the seventeenth century. Two venerable inns survive, there is a detectable high street, the old vicarage is a palatial house of the early sixteenth century, and a large timber-framed house stands in a hollow behind the main street. All the signs are that this was a village destined to become a town until something happened to thwart it.

The church, too, has an urban size and richness. It stands on its own hill, its red sandstone exterior refurbished with the battlements and pinnacles of the fifteenth-century Perpendicular fashion - usually a sign of local wealth. So it is all the more surprising to enter and find yourself in a nave that exemplifies unsophisticated Norman strength.

On the north side are the sturdy circular piers and plain single-step round arches of an early twelfth-century arcade. It makes an interesting contrast with the short arcade on the south side, which has the Gothic innovations of a century later - slender octagonal piers, tall pointed arches, and capitals carved imaginatively with heads, animals and leaves.

There are traces of wall painting all over the church, but what people come to see is the ambitious frieze over the north arcade. It has been dated to the very early thirteenth century, and bears an obvious similarity to the Bayeux Tapestry, showing horsemen engaged in combat. It is probably an allegorical illustration of

*A section of the painted frieze on the north arcade at Claverley church.*

the battle between the Christian virtues and pagan vices (one side is very definitely winning) so there should be seven on each side, and the likelihood is that it was originally continued along the west wall. Whatever its history it is a most vigorous painting of the kind that must have featured in many churches before the puritan fervour of the sixteenth century obliterated them.

The paintings were revealed during a careful restoration of 1902, and we can see another result by the organ, which is set into the tower. Here the restorers uncovered a Norman arch that proved the tower to be of a much earlier date than had been suspected. A gap has been left in the stonework to show a section of the well-preserved arch. The recess to the right of the organ, cut out of the tower buttress, is something of a mystery although it has been tentatively identified as a seat for penitents.

On the other side of the impressive chancel arch the church widens out strikingly to accommodate the chancel and its north and south chapels. The dominant feature is the big east window with imaginative curvilinear tracery that dates the chancel to the fourteenth century and the Decorated period. The north and south windows also show highly-original tracery.

The south chapel is obviously a later extension, with characteristic Perpendicular windows now carrying some dubious stained glass. Mounted on the east wall are two contrasting examples of Elizabethan incised memorials (there is an even earlier one just outside the chancel on the north wall of the nave). They both show married couples of the Gatacre family standing side by side, but there is a remarkable difference between the relaxed postures of the one (where the wife seems to be smiling slightly) and the stiff, stylised figures of the other, where eleven children have been perfunctorily sketched in at the bottom. Occupying another corner is an impressive tomb chest with alabaster effigies of Sir Robert Broke, once Speaker of the House of Commons, who died in 1558. He rests between his two wives, and eighteen children, mostly girls are shown below. A more modest tribute to Sir William Forbes Gatacre on the wall nearby is a roll-call of late nineteenth century campaigns.

The north chancel chapel is of less interest, but it contains a poignant reminder of the first world war - a wooden cross evidently retrieved from the battlefield and roughly inscribed with the name of Captain Gatacre, killed in 1916.

On the way out there is chance to examine one or two details at the west end. It would be interesting to know the artist responsible for the west window, with its unusual and rather fuzzy colour, and the smaller window in the same wall, which is much later and portrays in sentimental fashion a group of children with rabbits in attendance. Of the two fonts preserved here the larger is attractively decorated and obviously Norman, while the other is a simple tub that could well be Saxon.

It is always a pleasure to return to All Saints, partly because new details can be discovered on each visit, but also because there are few villages in Shropshire where the church occupies such a dominant, integral place.

## CLUN (ST. GEORGE)

*137: 300805*

When faced with a 'comments' column in a visitor's book most people are reduced to verbal poverty. But in the book at St. George's, amid the Beautifuls, Lovelys and Peacefuls, one visitor has written incisively *"I have never seen such exquisite kneelers"*.

Nor have I. There are dozens of them, magnificently embroidered with local scenes and glowing with colour. Whether they are by one person or many they are a fine modern contribution to ecclesiastical craftsmanship in a church where craftsmanship abounds.

If you park by the bridge in Clun you have a steep walk to the church, and by approaching from beneath you miss the impact of its powerful Norman tower topped by a later pyramid roof. This was the fortress-like structure that formed the first nucleus of the town. Shortly after it was built Robert de Say established his castle some distance to the north, thus ensuring that the town grew up on the other side of the river. These twin centres of interest, linked by an ancient pack-horse bridge, give Clun a highly individual character and great tourist appeal.

The squat church tower gives no clue to the interior of St. George's, which is large and sophisticated. Its present appearance owes much to the attentions of the famous G.E.Street, who carried out a major restoration in the 1870s, preserving most of the Norman work but smoothing out its rough strength. The original west doorway in the tower (a simple three-stepped arch) is still there, but nowadays you enter through an impressive porch, no doubt of the late fourteenth century but adorned by Street with an incongruous timber-framed gable.

*Clun church.
This watercolour of 1791 shows the thirteenth-century north aisle before the Victorian restoration.*

The two nave arcades catch the attention immediately. They are in the Transitional style of the late twelfth century - circular piers with big square capitals supporting pointed arches embellished with a simple zig-zag design. The arch by the pulpit is the odd one out - semicircular and obviously dating from some years earlier. There is no clear explanation for its presence. The arcades show that the church was extended by the addition of aisles very soon after its foundation, reflecting Clun's rapid early growth.

The splayed window high in the west wall proves that the tower was added to the nave. The small clerestory windows above the south arcade are almost as old; their purpose was to let in light when the aisles replaced the original nave walls, and an early clerestory like this is rare in Shropshire. The north wall of the nave has much-renewed lancets of the thirteenth century, while the south aisle was totally reconstructed by Street, who conscientiously maintained the Norman theme with small splayed windows (his version of a Norman doorway can be seen outside).

The roofs, both in the nave and the north aisle, have been considerably restored but remain fine examples of fifteenth-century design.

At the entrance to the chancel the pulpit is a well-preserved Jacobean piece with fully-carved panels and a sounding board. Most of the work beyond it is Victorian and rather grandly done, beginning with an impressive screen incorporating a design of intersecting tracery. There is further fine woodwork with complex carving in the stalls and organ case. For the chancel windows Street chose the restrained Early English style, so the east window consists of triple lancets with marble nook shafts reminiscent of the authentic examples in Acton Burnell church. The motif of the shafts is continued in the lancets to north and south and in the stone sedilia. The fittings were completed by a solid and dignified carved reredos. The only jarring note here is the choice of lurid green tiles for the sanctuary.

The north (Lady) chapel is of interest. Its panelling, which includes the reredos, has obviously been adapted from something else (box pews?) of the eighteenth century or earlier. The narrow east window is a strong, unpretentious representation of the Virgin and Child, and there is modern glass in the north window in memory of a former organist. (There is glass of the 1950s in two windows of the south aisle, inserted as memorials to Walter Bottomley.)

Before leaving, note the painting just inside the door. The work of an Ethiopian artist, it is a vigorous picture of St. George, and forms a memorial to Flight Sergeant Dermot Thesiger who died in 1942.

# CONDOVER (ST. MARY AND ST. ANDREW)

*126:494058*
*4 miles south of Shrewsbury off A49.*

The double dedication is probably explained by the presence of a separate chantry chapel in the fifteenth century with its own dedication to the Virgin Mary.

Like so many Shropshire churches this one served as both a place for common worship and a chapel for a local landowner. Seen from the road, the church appears to be an integral part of the village, but a walk round to the south side will reveal that it stands within a hundred yards of Condover Hall, the county's finest Elizabethan house. The Hall, now a school for blind and additionally-disabled children, was erected by Judge Thomas Owen in the 1580s for his son Roger.

As you approach the red sandstone church from the village street two very different styles become apparent. To the left is the gable end of an unadorned, rubble-built transept with Norman windows, while the porch and nave are built in a much fussier fashion. The explanation is that the central tower of the medieval church collapsed in 1660, resulting in a rebuilding of the western end. Very few churches were built in Shropshire in the later seventeenth century, and there appears to have been no agreed style, so the new work was something of a hotch-potch, and the architectural mix was complicated by the new porch of 1878, with its ogee arch and odd stepped gable. The tower, built in the 1670s, was given a more identifiable medieval look with lancet windows and battlements.

Inside the church the reconstruction was spectacular. The medieval nave and aisle were united as a very wide single space and spanned by a new piece of technology - a hammer-beam roof. This example is the most splendid in any Shropshire church, and was apparently hidden behind a plaster ceiling until 1878. The windows are definitely of the seventeenth century - almost straight-headed, with a simple pattern of tracery that gives the main lights alternate flat and arched heads.

The north transept was heavily renewed but retained its Norman windows - small, round-headed and widely-splayed. The east end, however, is all of the nineteenth century. The original thirteenth-century chancel was demolished in 1868 and replaced by a Victorian version of the Early English style - decent enough apart from the glass in the east window. Two interesting monuments remain here. In the south wall of the sanctuary are the alabaster effigies of an Elizabethan couple, assumed to be Thomas Scriven (died 1587) and his wife, while high on the wall a little to the west (and hard to see) is a memorial to Martha Owen (died 1641) in the new classical style.

*The chapel at Condover church. In the foreground is the statue of Sir Thomas Cholmondeley by G.F. Watts. Reginald Cholmondeley's effigy of his wife is on the left.*

When the chancel was rebuilt a north chapel was added, and it contains a remarkable group of monuments. On the north wall is a two-tier structure showing two pairs of stubby kneeling figures. The style, conventional in the late Elizabethan period, is a little old-fashioned for its 1641 date. The figures represent Bonham and Jane Norton at the top, while beneath are Jane's father, Judge Thomas Owen, and her brother Roger. The east wall is dominated by a flowing sculpture of 1746 by the celebrated Louis Francois Roubiliac, showing Roger Owen and his wife in classical draperies.

Equally famous was the artist George Frederick Watts, who was responsible for the dramatic kneeling figure on the south side of the chapel. The subject is Thomas Cholmondeley, who died on his honeymoon in 1864, having inherited the estate a year earlier. He wears a simple belted tunic and a cloak, the heavy folds of which are treated in masterly fashion.

But the most poignant mem-orial here is to the young Alice Cholmondeley, wife of Thomas's younger brother Reginald. She died in childbirth, and is shown lying with loosened hair and in a simple dress, holding her baby to her side. At her feet, in the place usually occupied by a dog on the tombs of knights, is an empty cradle. It is a rare and moving tribute by a husband to his wife, because the sculptor was Reginald Cholmondely himself.

## DIDDLEBURY (ST. PETER)

*137: 508854*
*4½ miles north-east of Craven Arms on B4368.*

The modern village of Diddlebury (pronounced Delbury) lies beside the road from Craven Arms to Much Wenlock. To find the old village centre you have to turn off and travel for half a mile - well worth the effort because it is a delightful place consisting of a few cottages, a farm, a school, a stream and the church, standing high up with the big house, Delbury Hall, behind it.

St. Peter's is surprisingly large and of ancient origin. The lower masonry of the tower has been tentatively identified as Saxon, although its general appearance is late Norman. The corner buttresses have been supplemented on the south side with two more of contrasting workmanship, no doubt as an early emergency measure.

The west doorway into the tower is a modest affair in a simple late-Norman style, but it obviously replaced a huge entrance, of which the flattened arch is still

*Diddlebury church.*

visible. There seems to be no explanation of why such an ambitious portal was constructed nor why it was so quickly blocked and replaced - unless, of course, the original scheme turned out to be a structural failure.

The north wall is of Saxon origin, a fact not evident from the exterior masonry, although the blocked north door is in the sturdy late Saxon style. An unusual feature of this wall is the series of memorial tablets, almost completely eroded and impossible to date; Holdgate church, a few miles away, also has examples. Was it a purely local custom? On the south side of the chancel a former priest's door has also been blocked by a large memorial.

On entering the church you can see that the north wall of the nave is almost entirely made up of herringbone masonry in blocks that have been quite carefully shaped for the purpose. A Saxon double-splayed window has also survived, and there is a later Norman window (now blocked) in the same wall. Set beneath this window are some fragments of very early, possibly Saxon, sculpture.

In the thirteenth century this original nave was enlarged by replacing the south wall with an arcade featuring the octagonal piers and pointed arches of the period, although the resulting aisle was virtually rebuilt during a restoration in the 1860s. The nave roof was probably installed at the same time, and it is difficult to see now whether the wooden heads on the corbels are medieval or Victorian copies. Rather oddly a row of wall tablets were set high on the arcade where they cannot possibly be read.

Although the general character of the chancel is Victorian the masonry is Norman. Two much-renewed windows of the period have been retained, and the outline of two more can be seen on either side of the present east window, which was inserted in the fourteenth century. The glass is fairly nondescript, although one chancel window has Victorian representations of St. Peter and St. Paul that appear to be caricatures but are perhaps an attempt at medieval pastiche. The other notable features are the tomb recesses with the ballflower ornament of the fourteenth century. Memorials abound, most of them heraldic, and the one on the south side of the sanctuary records John Fleming, who had thirteen sons and six daughters by the same wife. It seems to have been his only achievement. The thirteenth son was called Hercules.

## EATON UNDER HEYWOOD (ST. EDITH)

*137. 500900*
*4½ miles south-east of Church Stretton off B4371.*

St. Edith's is reached from Church Stretton by a series of narrow lanes, provided that you do not miss the minuscule signpost in Ticklerton.

*Opposite: The church at Eaton Under Heywood. The tower occupies an unusual position on the south-east side of the nave, probably as a result of the awkward site.*

Eaton must have been a settlement of some importance before and after the Norman invasion, but today there is just a large house (the old vicarage?) and a farm. All credit then to those who maintain the church so well and to the person who ensures that it is always open to visitors.

The approach road, passing through the embankment of the old Wenlock-Craven Arms railway, provides a fine view of the church, tucked beneath the wooded slopes of Wenlock Edge. Its dedication indicates that there was a Saxon church here - in fact it was a daughter church of Wenlock Abbey - and the precise site must have been of some significance because the Norman builders tackled its awkward contours again when there was no lack of flat ground nearby. The sharp slope resulted in two distinctive features - a tower on the south rather than the west side and an interior that inclines steeply towards the altar.

The sturdy tower was tidied up in the fifteenth century with neat battlements and finials, but otherwise it appears to be late Norman, with some unusually rich bell openings consisting of a single round-headed arch divided in two by a miniature pier with a carved capital.

Although the church has been restored at least twice the interior has not been Victorianised. The three small Norman windows in the nave have been renewed, but retain their authentic appearance, with the characteristic interior splays. The big three-light window in the north wall has the fine intersecting tracery of the fourteenth century and was no doubt an attempt to let in some badly-needed light. A splendid assemblage of reader's desk, pulpit and sounding board (incorporating some medieval carving) has fortunately survived from the seventeenth century, a precursor of the more elaborate three-decker arrangement that became popular a century later.

Only a step divides the nave from the chancel, which is of thirteenth-century origin, a fact which the restorers of 1869 acknowledged by providing three lancet windows in the east wall. But the roof is puzzling. A glance from the outside shows that the real roof is steeply-pitched, so this near-flat, panelled and embossed innovation was purely decorative in intent. How old is it? The design is of the fifteenth century, but false roofs were not a feature of that period. Without a ladder the question has to remain unanswered.

One feature here that can be firmly dated is the remarkable oak effigy on the north side, because it rests within a recess that has the ballflower decoration associated with the early fourteenth century. Above it is a decent if unexciting window designed by the Nicholson Studios in 1936 and showing St. Francis and St. George in statuesque poses. But the altar provides another surprise - the leaf motif on its front could have been done yesterday, yet it is shown in a very old photograph at the back of the church.

Several memorials commemorate members of the Pinches family of Ticklerton, but none of them has the eye-catching appeal of the ceramic tablet on the south wall of the chancel, in memory of Arthur Sparrow who died in 1893. It is a product of the late-Victorian 'arts and crafts' movement and similar to one in the church at Richards Castle. Among all the pious inscriptions it is refreshing to come across the splendidly defiant verse on the memorial to Joseph Matthews on the south wall of the nave:

*"Farewell vain world, I have had enough of thee*
*And little care I what thou sayest of me.*
*Thy smiles I court not nor thy frowns I fear,*
*My hope's in Christ, my head lies easy here."*

It ought to be the final memory for the visitor to take away. Unfortunately the last impression is likely to be of the garish west window, mercifully not in a position to dominate this fascinating church.

# Edstaston (St. Mary)

*126: 518320*
*2 miles north of Wem on B5476.*

Edstaston is a nondescript sort of place, and at first sight its church looks far from interesting. Driving past you would dismiss it as a Victorian creation, typically neat and prim. Only at close quarters does it become clear that St. Mary's is one of the best Norman churches in Shropshire.

It makes an interesting comparison with Heath chapel, its near-contemporary, which has sturdiness but no great refinement. St. Mary's is sophisticated by contrast and shows all the signs of having been built at the personal expense of a rich man rather than as a functional daughter church.

Start by walking through the churchyard to the north door. It has a three-stepped arch with some particularly elaborate scroll carving that incorporates tiny heads. The shafts on each side have rich capitals and the whole arch is completed by a carved hood-mould. The door itself, with its bold curvilinear ironwork, may well be original. At some time the doorway has become distorted, perhaps through ground movement or later building operations.

A few yards to the east is a Norman window, much larger than the usual minimal opening of the time, that obviously had meticulous care lavished on it by the craftsman who produced its miniature shafts and capitals, and the same is true of the smaller one lighting the chancel. (Note the anguished heads featured in the neighbouring window - not Norman but early medieval and no doubt intended as a salutary reminder of the terrors of Hell.)

On the south side another Norman door, originally leading into the chancel, is more simply constructed with one order of shafts and zig-zag decoration. But the masterpiece is the main south doorway, now the church entrance. This is a magnificent affair with a four-stepped arch, each step supported on a shaft with a carved capital and given a different form of geometrical decoration. Again there is

*The magnificient Norman south doorway at Edstaston church.*

ambitious ironwork wrought in curves and spikes on a door of great age.

The restoration that left the external masonry so featureless did not destroy the sense of antiquity inside. Here the nave is the centre of historical interest, not least because of the wealth of wall painting, now revealed centuries after being covered up by puritan reformers. Unfortunately most of it is tantalisingly indistinct, although the version of the Adoration of the Magi in the middle of the north wall has a clear figure that probably dates it to the early fourteenth century. The large painting over the north door is said to be a representation of St. Christopher, a popular subject, while that over the south door could be John the Baptist if the clear bare foot is anything to go by.

The remnants of interior string courses on the nave walls are a fairly rare Norman feature, as is a well-preserved recess in the north wall. A south window has a golden fragment of superior fifteenth-century glass at its head - another sign of a church continually well-endowed. And unless I was hallucinating there is a large owl made of painted wood perched on a north wall monument.

The chancel is of interest mainly because of the variety of windows, quite apart from the splayed Norman opening already studied from outside. The large east window is an impressive five-light structure with the intersecting tracery and elongated diamonds of the fourteenth century, and the south wall has a smaller example from the same period. The others have the stiff geometrical precision of fifteenth-century Perpendicular, and both were profusely embellished by a Victorian artist who did not know when to stop.

Glancing around for the last time it is nice to see that the finely-wrought Victorian oil lamps have been retained and adapted for electricity, but hard to understand why the font has been painted with representations of Prudence, Justice, Fortitude and Temperance - worthy virtues, of course, but not the ones most obviously associated with baptism.

# FRODESLEY (ST. MARK)

*126: 516011*
*7 miles south of Shrewsbury off A49*

If churches can be said to have personalities then St. Mark's at Frodesley is rather like the pessimist who has come to accept that bad luck is inevitable.

Situated on the Roman road that runs south-west from Wroxeter, it squeezes itself apologetically between a garden and the drive to Frodesley Hall, and you will need to look carefully for its unobtrusive iron gate. It was built in about 1809 as a simple rectangle of rubble sandstone, with a square, white-painted belfry. It had the tall, round-headed windows of that period and must have resembled the many nonconformist chapels built to the same plan in the 1830s.

*The unpromising appearance of Frodesley church conceals a very rewarding interior.*

Fifty years later, however, a north aisle was added, and it is hard to understand how it could have been done so tactlessly. Clamped against the side of the church like a lean-to shed, the extension was built in grey ashlar stone and in a vaguely Early English style completely at odds with the original structure. In recent years the church has suffered the added indignity of thick electrical cables clamped to its facade.

It is all rather discouraging, but the forlorn impression is dispelled immediately you step inside.

Ignore the north aisle with its dismal stained glass and concentrate on the original church, which is a perfect example of very early nineteenth-century work. The sturdy box pews and west gallery have survived. So have the windows in the south wall, big and clear and allowing a flood of light. The pulpit is hardly raised, and obviously encourages conversational discourse rather than declamation. Totally in keeping with the period (although it was no doubt installed later) is the small organ with its painted pipes.

Since this is a classical rather than a Gothic church there is no real chancel. The elegant communion rails simply divide the nave from the sanctuary - and you will not find a more beautifully crafted sanctuary in any small church in the county. Rich, dark wood panels line it on each side, flanking a reredos with fluted pilasters and discreet gold embellishment. The east end is further enriched by a glowing window created in the 1930s as a memorial to an incumbent. It is a strong and unsentimental portrayal of Christ as the Good Shepherd, standing in front of a stylised tree in silhouette.

It is a sobering thought that St Mark's is probably a candidate for redundancy. It is not famous and it stands within a diminished community. Economically it makes no sense, but its congregation obviously cares for it and it would be a tragedy if such a little-known gem were to disappear.

## HEATH CHAPEL

*137: 557856*
*8 miles north-east of Ludlow.*
*The key is at the first farm on the right along the road to the east.*

Many of Shropshire's parish churches originated as chapels or outposts of large parent churches. For the Normans it was a cost-effective way of catering spiritually for a scattered but rising population. As new settlements developed parishes became smaller and most of the chapels gained independent status. Heath Chapel, uniquely in the county, survived in its original state - tiny, unenlarged, apparently undedicated and only minimally altered in its structure. The village which it served is now a few humps in a neighbouring field, abandoned in the early middle ages, but the chapel survived and continued to serve a scattered population with no wealthy benefactors to finance ambitious restoration schemes.

The result is the nearest thing in Shropshire to an authentic Norman church. You reach it by narrow, winding lanes and find it in the middle of a field beside the road, a barn-like structure with no tower or bellcote and roofed now with modern tiles instead of the ragged thatch it must have had for centuries.

*The nave and chancel of Heath Chapel.*

Two striking features of the exterior are the pilaster buttresses typical of Saxon and early Norman buildings and the tiny windows that were the only source of light (the larger square one on the north side is a much later addition). Two of the windows are set into buttresses - an odd notion at first sight but making sense when you consider that it was easier to insert them into the dressed stone of the buttresses than into the rubble stonework of the walls. It must have been a cheap building, but it was nevertheless given a fine south doorway with two orders of shafts and much zig-zag decoration. Lacking a porch or the benefit of discreet restoration this doorway is now seriously eroded.

The interior is just a rectangle divided by a narrow chancel arch, double-stepped and with simple embellishment to the capitals. The walls are covered with old plaster, obviously concealing later wall paintings, and at the time of writing there is a proposal to restore them. Whether this is desirable is open to question. Wall paintings may be quaint but are seldom of aesthetic value, and their reappearance here would almost certainly detract from the stark Norman authenticity.

Much more worthy of preservation are the furnishings, because here we have a genuine example of how a remote country church of the seventeenth century was fitted out. Segregated in the chancel is the big 'squire's pew'. At the front of the nave are the rented box pews and at the back some rough benches for the servants. The low pulpit is combined with a reader's desk. The communion rails stand on three sides of the sanctuary in the approved puritan style. The font is a plain Norman tub.

And that is that. What cannot be conveyed in words is the atmosphere. There is no warmth, no richness here, just the cold and severe discomfort of a hermit's cell - a salutary reminder of the physical and spiritual hardiness of our ancestors.

## HODNET (ST. LUKE)

*127: 613286*
*5 miles south-west of Market Drayton on A53.*

The sandstone church at Hodnet is of impressive size, and its commanding position at the top of the village makes it even more imposing. The unique feature here is the low tower. The octagon was a favourite architectural form in the fourteenth century, but St. Luke's has the only totally octagonal tower in the county. It is a handsome structure with battlements that do not pretend to be anything but ornamental and generous bell openings that have the typical curvilinear tracery of the period.

*Opposite: The unique fourteenth-century octagonal tower of Hodnet church.*

The tower makes its presence felt as you enter, because its buttresses thrust their way rather brutally into the nave, which was also added in the fourteenth century. What is now the south aisle was the original Norman church, although the only clues are the remains of blocked Norman arches above the door and windows. Of the arcade that must have been built when the church was extended only two bays now remain at the east end - octagonal and with chamfered arches.

The organ was moved to the east end of the aisle in 1883, and it now stands behind an area of tiles laid to commemorate the church's most famous incumbent, the Revd. (later Bishop) Reginald Heber, rector from 1807 to 1823 and author of some famous hymns, including "From Greenland's Icy Mountains" and "Holy, Holy, Holy, Lord God Almighty". Although the organ adds nothing to the beauty of the church, it at least has the merit of subduing one of David Evans's usual showy windows.

As you move from here into the nave proper you are likely to be blinded by the huge Victorian east window, which has enormous impact but lacks an effective focus of interest, being made up largely of fussy patterns in colours that are excessively pretty for modern tastes. Against the light colours the imitation of intersecting tracery stands out starkly.

The window has the unfortunate effect of making its surroundings darker, although there is not much detail here to inspect. In fact the striking feature of such a spacious chancel is its lack of grandeur - the small and unpretentious altar lacks a reredos and is backed only by low panelling. The area is also extensively paved with shiny Minton tiles of the kind that tend to arouse hostility in some people, although when the colours are unobtrusive, as here, there is little to object to.

You will need to enter the sanctuary to view the Heber Percy Chapel, perhaps the best reason for visiting the church. It is an austere enclosure, with the Bishop

himself commemorated by a carved portrait in profile by the artist Francis Chantrey. In the centre of the chapel is the fine naturalistic effigy of Blanche Emily Heber, and anyone who has seen Reginald Cholmondeley's moving portrayal of his dead wife in Condover church will recognise the same hand at work. Cholmondeley was in fact Blanche's cousin.

The chapel was built in 1870, the year of Blanche's death, and after two disappointing windows it is worth studying the chapel's east window, where the glass is perhaps some of the best late-Victorian work in Shropshire. In four lights it represents various acts of charity. The figures are decisively drawn and coloured in a slightly stylised fashion that imparts great dignity. The nave is unremarkable except for some gigantic wall monuments, although the tower doorway at the back, presumably restored, is of interest since not many examples of this multi-stepped fourteenth-century style survive.

Among some interesting exhibits inside the door is a photograph of the church before the restoration of 1883. It shows the south aisle with a most elaborate pulpit arrangement that has now disappeared. Also on view is a collection of early books, including a Book of Hours of about 1450 and a 'Breeches Bible'.

Finally there is the font, a quaint lead-lined tub decorated with animals, birds and flowers. Surprisingly in view of its primitive appearance it turns out to be of seventeenth-century date - a very unlikely creation.

## HOLDGATE (HOLY TRINITY)

*137: 562896*
*8 miles south-west of Much Wenlock off B4378.*

These days Holdgate is nothing more than a small agricultural hamlet, but twenty years after the Norman conquest it had an important castle, and Henry I once came here to visit the lord of the manor. The church was built in the shadow of the castle, remains of which form part of a nearby farmhouse, and it underwent the usual process of development. Starting as a simple rectangular structure, it soon acquired a tower and, a century or so later, a more elaborate chancel.

The tower is of the no-nonsense Norman type. It has the customary fifteenth-century embellishments of battlements and pinnacles, but no effort seems to have been made at the same time to raise its height to more elegant proportions, so it remains almost cube-like in shape. By contrast the south doorway, one of the less well-known examples of its kind, is a very sophisticated piece of Norman work - the shafts have elaborate capitals and the three steps of the arch are each embellished with distinctive designs, including heavy zig-zag, an arch motif and beakheads. It is all contained within a hood-mould with different designs on its two halves.

There is no corresponding richness inside, where the nave has a rough austerity reinforced by a severe problem of creeping damp. The west wall, once the exterior wall of the church, retains a Norman splayed window, and at some point after the addition of the tower a lower triangular window was cut as a kind of peephole. The shape is characteristic of the thirteenth century. It is impossible to establish the age of the round-headed doorway into the tower without looking at the masonry behind the plaster, but given its off-set position it was probably a later access door rather than the original entrance to the church.

The font stands in a prominent position, and Holdgate is justifiably proud of it because many consider it the best in the county, with bold abstract carving that is typical of the most superior craftsmanship of the twelfth century. The benches may well be of the sixteenth century, and it is interesting to see that when box pews became fashionable some of the benches were converted by simply adding doors.

At the front of the nave on the south side is the splendid Cresset family pew, rather clumsily reassembled after being moved from its original position. Dating from the seventeenth century, it incorporates shafts and an elaborate heraldic canopy, and is perhaps unique for a Shropshire country church. The other unusual feature of the nave is the tomb recess in the south wall; these fourteenth-century

*The austere interior of Holdgate church. Behind the Victorian chancel arch are the original thirteenth-century east windows.*

features are common enough but are usually found in the chancel or in an external wall. Was it re-sited during restoration?

Restoration in the 1890s was certainly responsible for the new chancel arch, which is hardly in keeping with the character of the church. The chancel itself was treated more discreetly. Its thirteenth-century origin is indicated by the two lancets in the east wall, but the windows to north and south of the sanctuary are of a century later - one has somehow lost its tracery. Another lancet on the north side has glass of the 1920s representing a rather striking Virgin and Child with a homely English landscape in the background.

It is an attractively unpretentious interior with its own particular air of antiquity, but it cannot be easy for a small community to maintain a church of its size, so when you visit it be generous with your donation. And before you leave walk round to the south side of the chancel to look at the sheila-na-gig on the wall. There are several of these female fertility figures on churches in the area - a reminder of the cautious English tradition of invoking pagan as well as Christian traditions just to be on the safe side. It is remarkable that the rather rude heathen figures have survived periods of prudery. This one is so eroded that it cannot possibly offend, and to see a fairly complete example you must go to Church Stretton.

## HUGHLEY (ST. JOHN THE BAPTIST)

*137: 565980*
*5 miles south-west of Much Wenlock off B4371.*

The descent from Wenlock Edge provides an aerial view of Hughley, a classic Shropshire hamlet isolated among flat green fields. Once the centre of a small farming community (there is still at least one active farm) it has now become something of a gentrified retreat, although at the time of writing it is reassuring to see that its outstanding building, the timber-framed manor house, remains authentically unrestored.

The unpretentious church stands on its small plot, screened by yews. Its one slight eccentricity is a timber-framed belfry with red brick infilling, which proved something of an embarrassment to A.E.Housman, who endowed the church with a spire in one of his poems.

The nave has a north wall of the thirteenth century, and its windows are of some interest because they represent the post-Norman Transitional period when the first Gothic influences were creeping in. Consequently the windows are quite large and pointed in the new fashion but still have the deep splays of the Norman period.

But the great attraction here is the chancel screen. It would not cause much excitement in Herefordshire or the southern Welsh border where magnificent screens are commonplace, but in Shropshire it is a rarity. Its lower section consists of panels pierced by squares carved in a design familiar from the tracery of fifteenth-century windows, yet the top of the frame holding the panels has a pattern of quatrefoils, a motif of a century earlier. The upper structure is an elegantly-curving canopy with carved panels reminiscent of the type of roof vaulting introduced in the fourteenth century. The canopy is completed by intricately-worked designs that include birds and flowers, and the whole screen is fringed with the same scrupulous delicacy. The workmanship is that of a skilful local craftsman rather than a highly-paid master.

The church has other rewarding details. The chancel east window is a fine example of fourteenth-century curvilinear tracery and contains medieval glass in

*The fine chancel screen at Hughley, probably of the early fifteenth century.*

which a blue grinning devil stands out sharply and disturbingly. There is more jumbled medieval glass in the north chancel window. To the right of the altar a large female head once served as the base for a statue. The sanctuary also has a fairly rare feature - a 'pillar piscina' like a miniature font. Note too the medieval tiles on the chancel floor.

St. John's was obviously never a church with wealthy gentry to endow it. Its humble status is perhaps best indicated by the lack of assertive monuments; there are just three - two of them tributes to former priests and the third commemorating two soldiers who died in the first world war.

## IRONBRIDGE (ST. LUKE)

The Church Building Act of 1818 permitted a million pounds of taxpayers' money to be expended on new churches in areas where they were lacking - mainly in the industrial towns which were developing with astonishing speed, but also in the extensive new residential suburbs that were a feature of most large towns. The funding was necessary because these areas lacked the traditional sources of money (in particular the philanthropy of major landowners) that had ensured the building and maintenance of churches in rural parishes.

The money was administered by Commissioners who were not unduly generous. £20,000 was considered enough for a new church with a potential congregation of two thousand, and many were built with a budget of half that sum, helped by private contributions or sometimes by a levy on local rates. Nevertheless, it was an unprecedented gesture by the Government, even if some cynics saw it not as a pious act but as a calculated attempt to fight back against the Nonconformist churches, which were achieving great strength in the industrial regions.

As well as imposing tight budgets the Commissioners also restricted architectural freedom. As a general principle churches were to be built *"with a view to accommodating the greatest number of persons at the smallest expense within the compass of an ordinary voice, one half of the number to be free seats for the poor."* More detailed requirements were laid down: *"The site must be central, dry and sufficiently distant from factories and noisy thoroughfares...the windows ought not to resemble modern sashes, but whether Grecian or Gothic, should be in small panes and not costly...The pulpit should not intercept a view of the altar, but all seats should be placed so as to face the preacher. We should recommend pillars of cast iron for supporting the gallery of a chapel...Ornament should be neat and simple, yet variable in character..."*

In 1818 the classical style of church building - a rectangular auditorium with no division between nave and chancel and with the altar completely open to view - was widely accepted, but during the twenty years that followed there was increasing pressure for a return to medieval Gothic. As a result many architects were faced with the task of accommodating the Commissioners' specifications for an open auditorium inside a building that had at least a vaguely Gothic appearance.

*Ironbridge church.*

A grasp of all these constraints will help us to understand St Luke's, Ironbridge, one of the few Commissioners' churches in Shropshire. It was built in the mid-1830s, by which time Ironbridge had developed into a formless community strung out along the Severn gorge - a conglomeration of hovels, cottages, mansions, pubs, iron furnaces, wharves, warehouses and workshops. Although grander houses were being built high on the hill, the physical limitations of the gorge meant that few could escape the clamour of industry and the rumble of heavy cart traffic. No-one had offered to provide a church, probably because the people in a position to do so were predominantly Nonconformist (there was no lack of chapels at the eastern end of the town) and there was no acknowledged leading family with social responsibilities. (Nevertheless, the Quaker Abraham Darby III saw it as his duty to provide an Anglican church in Coalbrookdale.)

So Ironbridge was a prime candidate for the Commissioners' money, and local architect Thomas Smith of Madeley was commissioned. But where was the church to be placed to conform with the stipulation that the site should be *"central, dry and sufficiently distant from factories and noisy thoroughfares"*? The town centre was at the Iron Bridge, an area not only very noisy indeed but already full of buildings. The only possible compromise was a platform site above the market place, partly cut out of the bank and partly built out artificially, with room for a notional graveyard at the west end. Unfortunately this platform obstructed the precipitous steps from the market place to the upper road, so a tunnel was constructed to allow the steps to pass beneath the graveyard.

There was, of course, plenty of local expertise available to solve problems like this, and the site has a characteristic air of nonchalant confidence that can be slightly unconvincing to the modern visitor who sees the church perched at the extreme edge of a steep drop.

In his design Smith opted for a discreet compromise of styles. He used yellow brick to produce a building that has vestiges of the classical tradition - a basic rectangle and a symmetrical western entrance front reminiscent of Telford's church at Madeley - but which incorporates Gothic features like paired lancet windows and a tower with battlements and finials. As required the windows have small panes, but there is a decorative touch in the elongated lozenge shape of the glazing bars.

The space beneath the tower acts as an antechamber, with stairs to the gallery, which is a dominant feature of the interior. Occupying three sides and supported on cast-iron columns, it is spacious and economically designed with a wood-panelled front. In a conservative church of this date one would have expected the organ to be placed in the west gallery, but the gallery has a central access door, which seems to indicate that the organ's present position is the original one. The space which it occupies is matched on the south side by the vestry, so perhaps this symmetrical arrangement was indeed planned from the start, in which case the church was in the vanguard of the new fashion for chancel choirs.

Not that there was much of a chancel - the big arch really marks off the sanctuary, and the present arrangement of choir stalls is a modern adaptation, formed of Victorian stalls which have obviously been imported. The east window, of stepped lancets in the thirteenth-century manner, was given heavily-coloured glass in the later Victorian years; the effect is rich, but it detracts from the airy lightness intended by the builder.

The overall impression of St. Luke's is exactly what might be expected of a Commissioners' church - cheaply built and designed with an eye to accommodating a large number of people in a limited space. Yet the interior has the elegance produced by pleasing proportions, and, like other buildings in the district, it is a reminder that in the early nineteenth century educated taste was applied even to the most functional structures.

## LANGLEY CHAPEL

*126: 537011*
*1½ miles south of Acton Burnell.*

The enthusiast for historic churches often has reason to be grateful for apathy and negligence. A short drive along narrow lanes to the south of Acton Burnell brings you to a barn-like building standing alone in a field. It is the Langley Chapel, so called because it was the tiny place of worship for the household of Langley Hall, long since demolished and marked now by a few remains at the nearby farm.

*Langley Chapel: the reader's desk, from which the minister conducted the services.*

These days the chapel is a scheduled monument, signposted by English Heritage and equipped with the usual interpretation boards, but its rescue came at the end of nearly two centuries of neglect. When the Hall was abandoned nobody bothered about the chapel, so it has survived as a remarkable illustration of puritan worship.

It appears to have been built in 1564, a rare date for a church building. It is a simple rectangle of big ashlar stone blocks with a weatherboarded belfry and stone roof tiles. Its windows show no architectural consistency; one is straight-headed in the Elizabethan fashion, another is arched and a third is pointed, while the big east window appears to be a copy of the thirteenth-century west window at Acton Burnell.

English Heritage have wisely left the interior as they found it. The west end is occupied by rough benches of excruciating design, no doubt occupied by the servants. Right at the back is a pew apparently intended for a small choir or band. Towards the front are box pews for the family, draughtproof but hardly more comfortable. It is easy to imagine the small congregation sitting here in agonising postures while the service was read from the huge, roofed reader's desk and lengthy sermons issued from the portable pulpit.

The puritan tradition made no provision for an altar. Here we have a small, plain communion table with kneeling desks surrounding it on three sides. (This was something of a concession; in more radical churches the sacrament was received sitting or standing in order to avoid any hint of idolatry.) An unexpected feature is the chancel paving of medieval tiles. They must have been brought from somewhere, and the most obvious source is Acton Burnell church, because they match those in the north transept there.

The Langley Chapel is a fortunate survival - draughty, cheerless and altogether fascinating.

## LLANYBLODWEL (ST. MICHAEL)

*126: 239229*
*6 miles south-west of Oswestry off B4396.*

Llanyblodwel church simply could not happen in this age of ecclesiastical regulations and red tape. When the Revd. John Parker arrived in 1845 he found the old church in a dangerous condition with the south wall close to collapse. He at once offered to superintend its repair, and one thing led to another so that between 1845 and 1855 the church was almost completely remodelled to his highly individual taste.

The church stands outside the village centre in a tranquil position on a plateau above the river Tanat, and the first inkling of its unconventional design is the sight of its bullet-shaped tower and spire. (This does not seem to have been a flight of fancy but a shape calculated to provide the maximum strength and durability.)

The south wall is entirely Parker's work. It features prominent brick-faced buttresses, dormers and three windows with elongated tracery. A walk round to the east end shows the gables of the nave and north aisle, of equal size and containing the only two original windows, which are severely Perpendicular in style. Continuing the circuit of the church you pass the north wall - definitely 'the back', with a rather unfinished look - and arrive at the foot of the tower.

Detached from the west wall with a short connecting passage, it is finely constructed and must have demanded considerable skill.

As you enter the church through a plain Norman door the interior seems at first sight totally bewildering - the dark woodwork, the coloured paint and the patterns and texts that cover almost every surface create a visual jumble and camouflage the

*Some of the Revd. John Parker's embellishments at Llanyblodwel.*

layout. In fact the space is divided between a nave and a shorter north aisle of equal width, separated by a three-bay arcade. This has stubby octagonal piers supporting wide arches and looks much older than its fifteenth-century date.

At the back of the nave Parker's gallery is unusual in being free-standing, supported all round by quatrefoil piers with carved capitals and containing much elaborate woodwork. The roof conforms to the spirit of the Perpendicular period, being flat and set on short arch braces rising from corbels. A wooden grid divides it into panels with bosses. Towards the front, and for no apparent reason, there is a single heavily-decorated hammer-beam truss.

It is hard to spot a surface that has not received its share of decoration. Texts abound on the walls and above the arcade, the window embrasures are patterned and much of the stonework is painted.

The same decoration continues into the shallow chancel, reached through a much-restored fifteenth-century screen, and is echoed in the altar, which has a wooden front fretted with white tracery and embellished with miniature buttresses. This motif appears again in the multi-coloured reredos, capped by stylised roof tiles. Nothing is predictable here - the communion rails, for example, are composed of a substantial wooden frame holding variously carved panels.

To the north the chancel is extended to form a chapel containing two formidable wall monuments. The larger of the two (1752) is very imposing indeed (so is the inscription) and is the work of the famous sculptor J.M. Rysbrack. Another screen separates this chapel from the north aisle, notable mainly for a low choir gallery and for the pictures of former incumbents, including John Parker himself.

Whether you love or hate the eccentricities of this church there is no denying its fascination. It was too much for a later generation, who covered up the decorations and gave the interior a much more conventional character, and we owe a debt to the parishioners and the craftsmen who, in 1960, took on the task of revealing Parker's exuberance once more.

# Longnor (St. Mary)

*126: 488005*
*7 miles south of Shrewsbury on A49.*

St. Mary's stands just inside the park of Longnor Hall, and there is a well-defined path from that fine late seventeenth-century house. (The original house would have been considerably nearer.) At the same time the church is very much part of the village. It is a situation repeated in many Shropshire parishes, emphasising the close historical relationship between the county's landowning families (in this case the Corbets) and their communities.

The exterior of the church, which has been only lightly restored, is an important example of Early English building. The estimate of its date is between 1260 and 1280, and the east window is characteristic of the time, with three stepped lancets surmounted by circles. The rows of smaller lancets on each side of the chancel are reminiscent of those of the same period at Acton Burnell, though not nearly as rich in their embellishment.

*Longnor church in its parkland setting. The authentic-looking west window is a Victorian copy in wood of the east window.*

The external staircase leading to the west gallery is an unusual sight, but a sensible enough solution to the difficulty of very limited space inside. No doubt it was an eighteenth-century addition. As you enter by the new west door the area under the gallery is certainly claustrophobic, and you can see the sense in blocking off the former north and south doors and substituting the unusual semi-glazing with intersecting tracery.

Within this Early English shell

the little nave gives a strong impression of eighteenth-century seemliness. The box pews remain, and there are cavernous pews at the front for Squire and Rector, the latter having access to a very elevated pulpit. The tiny organ is also perfectly in keeping, although it was installed as recently as 1976. But the odd sight of a piscina in front of the pulpit is puzzling. It was uncovered in 1980, and suggests the presence of an earlier altar, but there is no evidence of an older church on the site. The alternative explanation - that there was once a second altar here - seems equally unlikely in such a small church.

The lack of family monuments, apart from discreet memorials to Victorian Corbetts on each side of the altar, is a little surprising but fortunate. A lavish display of mortuary art could easily have ruined the appearance of this elegant fusion of the thirteenth and eighteenth centuries. The congregation is obviously proud of it. It is beautifully kept and (thank goodness) always open to visitors.

## LUDLOW (ST. LAURENCE)

The thrusting, arrogant tower of St. Laurence's dominates the approaches to Ludlow, but the church has an annoying habit of disappearing once you reach the town centre, and it is necessary to find the narrow passage behind the Buttercross that takes you to its gates.

Guides to the church are rather daunting in their complexity, but this is because of the many detailed features on view for the visitor who is prepared to make a leisurely tour. The architectural history of the church is quite straightforward. The original Norman building was rebuilt in 1199, and much of the masonry of the south wall dates from this time. In the early thirteenth century the unusual hexagonal porch was added - one of only three in the country - together with a deep chancel. The early fourteenth century saw the construction of a new north aisle and the south transept, and later in the century the north transept was added.

It was during the prosperous fifteenth century that the church was radically altered in the Perpendicular style that now gives it its character.

The most obvious manifestation of that style is the tower, 135 feet high and out of proportion to the general height of the church. It was an ostentatious symbol of wealth and given every Perpendicular refinement, including the stepped and polygonal corner buttresses ending in turrets and finials, battlements, immensely tall lower windows and bell openings that are incorporated into window shapes largely made up of blind panels.

*A nineteenth-century view of the south side of Ludlow church,showing the uncleared churchyard.*

It is worth examining the interior of the two-storey porch (probably dating from the years 1300-1320) because Shropshire has comparatively few examples of roofs with early rib vaulting. Here the ribs meet at a central boss. The windows have the restrained curvilinear tracery of the early Decorated period, before the development of much freer patterns later in the century.

The interior transformation of the fifteenth-century becomes strikingly apparent as you enter the nave. It is a vista of soaring arches, the two arcades closed off by the splendid west tower arch. The arches give the impression of plain severity, but closer inspection reveals complex moulding. The grandiose effect is enhanced by the sheer height of the nave, and by its low-pitched timber roof, embellished with panels and bosses and supported by arch braces rising from elaborate corbels in the walls. (In a church on which little expense was spared one might have expected a stone vaulted roof, but there was a stubborn loyalty to the timber tradition in Shropshire.)

The various guides to the church (David Lloyd's pamphlet in the 'Historic Ludlow' series is recommended) point out the small details, and this account will be confined to major architectural features, beginning in the north aisle.

This is where most of the early fourteenth-century work survived, and it shows most clearly in the windows. The row of six in the north wall demonstrate the beginnings of the transition from Early English simplicity to the free style of the Decorated period. The arches are cusped, and the heads consist of a circle surrounding a cinquefoil design - containing original glass in the three windows on the right. The aisle west window is of particular interest because it contains the ballflower decoration characteristic of the early fourteenth century.

As you move towards the tower you encounter two half-arches, actually tower buttresses, and between them the organ now occupies the north transept. Earlier organs had been situated above the rood screen, but in accordance with Victorian custom this one was rebuilt here in the 1860s.

There is now a chance to look closely at the piers supporting the tower. They are in a rough diamond shape and as massive as anything the Normans produced, but the elaborate shafting and moulding removes any sense of primitive functionalism. The huge four-light windows of the tower, already viewed from outside, are surmounted by a finely-crafted timber roof.

On the other side of the half-arches, and entered by a delicate fifteenth-century screen, is St. John's Chapel, formerly the chapel of the powerful Palmers' Guild. The eye is drawn at once to the east end, where the altar canopy and the window are both original, the latter a well-restored representation in eight lights of a local

*The impressive Perpendicular nave, tower crossing and chancel of Ludlow church.*

legend involving the Ludlow Palmers, Edward the Confessor and St. John. There is another fine window of the same period on the north side, showing the Annunciation in the upper lights and St. Catherine, John the Baptist and St. Christopher below. The north wall panelling is original.

The adjacent chancel is eighty feet long and rises to another outstanding timber roof of five bays, richly panelled and embossed. Nothing illustrates the technological advances of the final Gothic period better than the vast east window, a multi-light structure showing scenes from the life of St. Laurence, but of equal interest is the adjacent window in the south wall, which illustrates six of the Commandments and is a unique survival in England.

The sedilia, piscina and large Easter sepulchre (now a tomb recess) are all characteristic of the fifteenth century, but the elaborate reredos is almost entirely a Victorian copy. The stalls are famous for the carvings of their misericords, while the rood screen is a rare example in the county of the two-bay type with a loft above.

The Lady Chapel is entered through another handsome screen. The string course in the wall is a reminder that the masonry of this south side of the church is Norman in origin. The dominant feature is the big Jesse window (a representation of Christ's geneaology stemming from Jesse) which looks authentically medieval but is in fact an almost complete restoration by the firm of Hardman. The reticulated window tracery dates it to the first half of the fourteenth century.

The south transept and south aisle are not of great architectural significance, although they contain features of antiquarian interest.

St. Laurence's church is so rich in detail that successive visits are necessary to absorb it all, but as you pause at the door to take a last look the prevailing impression is plain enough. At the time when the town reached its medieval peak of prosperity the technology existed to translate that prosperity into wood, stone and glass. Fortunately the architectural taste of the time dictated that it should be done in a chaste and disciplined manner, so Shropshire's grandest parish church became a thing of genuine beauty rather than an exuberant temple for nouveaux riches tradesmen.

## MELVERLEY (ST. PETER)

*126: 333166*

You approach Melverley by way of roads that grow progressively narrower, and when you are brought up short on the edge of the river Vyrnwy you find the church. The river runs a few feet from its foundations, which have been constantly threatened over the years by the erosion of the bank, but a recent special appeal for funds received a widespread response and the church seems safe for the moment.

It is certainly worth saving. Shropshire's only timber-framed parish church, it is reputed to have been built at the beginning of the fifteenth century, and the close studding of the frame appears to confirm it. (Later timber-framed buildings in Shropshire, unless built for very rich clients, tended to have square-panel construction.) Apart from its small belfry there is nothing distinctively ecclesiastical about it - any house or barn would have been built in the same way. The present windows are later additions, inserted at various times to replace the tiny apertures that no doubt served the original church, and it is interesting to see that although the building conforms to no formal architectural pattern the Victorian restorers conscientiously gave their east window a Perpendicular style appropriate to the church's age (the stained glass could hardly be less appropriate).

The interior is divided into three sections by partitions that are integral to the structure. At the west end, entered by a door that could well be original, is a lobby with drunkenly distorted stairs leading to a tiny gallery above. There is some evidence that this is an Elizabethan addition. From here you pass into the main

*The east end of Melverley church.*

body of the church, divided into nave and chancel by a heavily-framed screen that incorporates the tie-beam of the roof.

The sparse furnishings are of later date than the building, apart from the octagonal font, which is crude enough to be the sole relic of the earlier church. The altar is a small, portable communion table of the kind adopted in Elizabethan Protestant churches (another example can be seen at the Langley Chapel). The lectern, to which the Bible is chained, dates from the eighteenth century, while the pulpit is a rather fine Jacobean piece with carved panels. The Victorian oil lamps have been preserved, though adapted to electricity, and so has the curly brass chandelier over the chancel. The only other feature of note is a charming eighteenth-century monument with a naive verse in memory of Richard and Margaret Downes.

*Opposite: Melverley church: a view of the interior from the gallery.*

These bits and pieces of different ages serve to emphasise the remarkable continuity of the church's history. Shropshire has many older parish churches than this, but none so fragile, and it is surprising that the restoration of 1878 was done with such a light hand. In fact it is surprising that restoration took place at all, since the late nineteenth century was not a period noted for zeal in conserving ancient buildings, and a brand new church could easily have been built on a safer site. Perhaps the explanation is that Melverley was simply not considered important enough. It never really formed part of the rural community and for most of its life was a haphazard settlement serving the river traffic - the Severn is only a short distance away. Hence the name of the nearby Tontine Inn. There is another of the same name on the wharf at Ironbridge, and both commemorate a form of primitive insurance policy favoured by boatmen. The village would have been dying in 1878, no doubt to cries of 'good riddance' from its more genteel neighbours.

Nowadays the old village consists of a few scattered houses. But its church survives, and fortunately there are enough people to care for it and ensure that this unique building at the end of nowhere continues to be a place of pilgrimage for visitors from all over the world.

## MINSTERLEY (HOLY TRINITY)

*126: 375050*
*10 miles south-west of Shrewsbury on A488.*

Holy Trinity came into being in the late 1680s as a chapel-of-ease to the parish of Westbury. It was an act of private philanthropy by the owners of Minsterley Hall, and by employing the London builder William Taylor the benefactors obtained a church that must have astonished this part of rural Shropshire. Holy Trinity is significant not only because very few churches were being built outside London at that time but also because its design incorporated features that were distinctly avant-garde in the provinces.

In the national context it is contemporary with Wren's innovative classical churches in London, and with the first flowering of the English Baroque style as displayed at Chatsworth and Castle Howard. Locally it represents a very early (possibly the first) Shropshire venture into what has become known as 'provincial Baroque' - a style displayed a few years later in large houses such as Cound Hall and Kinlet Hall. The characteristics of provincial Baroque were the use of brick with stone dressings and the incorporation of classical features like columns, pilasters and pediments in an ostentatious and flamboyant manner.

Taylor was probably not an architect but a builder who had picked up an inkling of this Baroque fashion in the course of his work on new houses in other parts of the country, and his church at Minsterley has all the signs of an experimental project. Using a limited budget, he followed the principles of Wren and others in producing a plain rectangle with no structural division between nave and chancel. The walls lean in slightly for no discernible reason and are supported by an array of vestigial buttresses, some bearing fat rainwater pipes in lead. The basic brick structure is relieved by stone dressings to the windows, which are large, round-headed and plentiful, with carved cherubs in the keystones.

But the astonishing tour-de-force is the west facade, a showy and bizarre assembly of fanciful components with no classical authority whatsoever. A segment-headed doorway is flanked by rusticated pilasters and surmounted by an array of naive carving. Above this is an elaborate window with carved pilasters and capitals, and above this again a stone slab holding a clock. Symmetry is provided by four more rectangular windows, and the whole composition is framed within a big segmental arch supported on giant rusticated pilasters. The square belfry is perched above the facade and is embellished with balusters and triangular pediments on all four sides.

*The unique baroque west front of Minsterley church.*

You enter the church through a south porch and a heavy panelled oak door, and the first impression is one of light. It streams through the five big windows on each side of the nave, and this alone must have been a novelty for the first congregations here, accustomed to the dim mystery of a Gothic church. The west end of the nave has now been turned into a 'social area' (the subject of an indignant comment in the visitors' book) but the only innovation that detracts from the total effect is the sealing off of the balustraded west gallery. Fortunately the homely distorted woodwork of the gallery front is still visible, a reminder of the local timber-frame tradition of building.

The east end of the nave is dominated by a splendid pulpit with a sounding board in the form of an ogee-shaped dome. A distinctive piece of eighteenth-century work, it was brought here when Westbury church was restored and modernised, and the same may be true of the low, gated chancel screen. This would certainly not have formed part of the original furnishings, although it fits happily enough to the modern eye.

The church's fine woodwork continues in the sanctuary with the slender communion rails and a reredos which is flanked by tall panels headed by segmental pediments. The panels now hold modern tapestries, but would have been inscribed originally with the Lord's Prayer and the Ten Commandments. They are an authentic classical feature, although it is worth noticing that the east window was given Y-tracery - a slight concession to older Gothic taste. Holy Trinity was fortunate in not acquiring pious pictorial glass in the Victorian period, something which would certainly have upset Taylor's attempt at austere elegance.

From the antiquarian point of view the church is best known for its collection of maiden's garlands or 'virgins' crowns' hanging from the west gallery. Their exact significance has been disputed, but it seems to be agreed that they were carried at the funerals of unmarried women and hung in the church afterwards. Constructed in the form of a crown, they featured paper flowers and symbolic representations of white gloves. They must once have been a common sight in churches, but their fragility ensured that few survived, and Minsterley's collection of seven dating from the eighteenth century is perhaps explained by the fact that the church has never undergone major restoration.

The reaction of the first Minsterley congregation to their new chapel is not recorded, but it is likely that the culture-shock was considerable. Even today Holy Trinity has an air of modernity, the effect perhaps of its restrained interior which lacks obvious period features. (The contrast between the exuberant facade and the plain interior may possibly be explained not so much by taste as by shortage of money!) What is certain is that the architectural importance of Minsterley church, both locally and nationally, is greatly underrated.

## MORETON CORBET (ST. BARTHOLOMEW)

*126: 562232*
*5 miles south-east of Wem on B5063.*

The famous attractions at Moreton Corbet are the ruins of the medieval castle and of Andrew Corbet's innovative Elizabethan mansion, but the nearby church should really not be missed.

From the outside it looks unremarkable. It is dressed in respectable grey stone and the only unusual features are the odd corner embellishments at the top of the tower (the upper section was replaced in the eighteenth century) and a strange west window in the shape of a spheric triangle with similar tracery within it. This is similar to one in the west chapel wall at Alberbury and is an outstanding example of inventive work of the Decorated period.

The interior is full of interest. You enter through the tower and emerge into a plain Norman nave, much restored. The eye is taken immediately by the glowing colours of the east window (1905), the work of the distinguished artist Sir Ninian Comper, who also designed the unusual reredos. This has two delicately-carved figures portraying the Annunciation, but more unusually it incorporates two elephants, heraldic symbols of the Corbets. The chancel ceiling is splendidly painted and features, over the altar, a gilded canopy studded with heraldic devices. A tiny splayed window in the north wall is a reminder of the church's Norman origins.

A squint on the south side of the chancel allowed worshippers in the south aisle to see the altar. This aisle, added in the mid-fourteenth century, is vast, equalling the nave in size. The west window shines with stained glass, but it cannot compete

*Moreton Corbet church. In the foreground is the eighteenth-century 'squire's pew' attached to the large south aisle.*

with the stunning east window - a creation of the late 1890s representing Christ receiving the children. It is huge, delicately-coloured and teeming with figures, including children of all ages (see back cover).

Immediately in front of it is a tall chest tomb bearing the effigies of Sir Robert Corbet (died 1513) and his wife. They are conventionally portrayed, but the carved figures around the chest are puzzling. Normally one would expect the children to be shown here. Were there really eighteen of them? They are certainly not the usual bland afterthoughts but finely-detailed and doll-like. A similar tomb against the west wall shows Sir Richard Corbet (died 1567) and wife, though their chest bears heraldic motifs, including owls and the elephants again. Unexpectedly the centre panel shows a baby.

Built into the south wall, and railed off from the aisle, is the extraordinary room that constituted the Corbet family pew. Designed for comfort, it has a fireplace in one corner and carved seating on three sides. In another corner is the overblown monument to Richard Corbet (died 1691), very much in the new classical fashion with a bust framed by fluted pilasters and an open segmental pediment.

This fascinating church is redolent of the powerful Corbet family, so it is fitting that the first and last monument to seize the attention is the sculpture commemorating Vincent Corbet, who died aged 13. Completed in 1904, it stands at the church gate and is a lively bronze figure by I.H.M. Furse.

## MORVILLE (ST. GREGORY)

*138: 670939*
*3 miles west of Bridgnorth on A458.*

St. Gregory's is a simple church of rubble construction with a plain Norman tower, and it would deserve inclusion in the book if only because of its fine situation. It stands in open parkland, facing the wide frontage of Morville Hall, an Elizabethan mansion remodelled in the eighteenth century and provided with symmetrical service wings detached from the house.

But it is also of architectural interest because it is possible to see inside two stages of Norman building. The rather primitive chancel arch, slightly flattened and simply decorated with a face on one capital and a fruit on the other, is probably a survival of the church which is known to have been consecrated in 1118. The arcades, however, are far more sophisticated and are part of the improvements carried out after the church became a daughter foundation of Shrewsbury Abbey in about 1140. They are still round-headed but have quite complex piers - square with shafts attached on each side and with carved capitals in various designs.

A window in the nave south wall has the typical interior splay of the Norman period, and there is another high in the west wall. The west door has the date 1118 carved confidently over it, and indeed it is likely to be the original entrance against which the tower was built a little later.

The chancel now looks very Victorian, although much of the masonry is Norman and the side windows have the distinctive flat heads of the sixteenth century. One window on the north side of the sanctuary incorporates fourteenth-century glass showing the Crucifixion, but two of the others were given rather feeble representations of saints in the nineteenth century.

*Morville church. The original section of the tower has Norman pilaster buttresses and lancet windows; the new top, added much later, can be seen clearly.*

The church has its curiosities. The carved wooden plaques on the arcades, for example, show the four evangelists, but their date and origin are uncertain. They have the look of the Oberammagau carving that was introduced into several churches during the nineteenth century, but no doubt someone will write to tell me either that they are medieval or that they were made recently by a local craftsman. There is no doubt about the antiquity of the wooden chest at the back of the church, carved out of a single log, nor about the font, which is a Norman tub elaborately incised with designs that include faces.

Notice, as you leave, the ironwork of the south door - with its sprawling curves it could well be the original late Norman ironmongery.

# ONIBURY (ST. MICHAEL)

*137: 456792*
*5 miles north-west of Ludlow on A49.*

For drivers on the A49 Onibury is a place to hurry through in case the lady in the signal box flashes the red lights and brings the barriers down. The penalty for being caught is a seemingly endless wait before the two-coach train lumbers apologetically through. But Onibury is a pleasant little Onny-side settlement and deserves better than to be thought of as a nuisance. If you turn off on to the lane behind the former station you will find a bustling village school and a coursed-rubble church standing within a well-tended churchyard.

There is nothing particularly distinguished about St. Michael's, and the only reasons for drawing attention to it are its thoroughly likeable character and the fact that it is exceptionally well cared for. From the outside it looks all of a piece, but its sturdy tower was added in the fourteenth century to a much older nave and chancel. What first catches the eye inside is a flattened and rather crude Norman chancel arch with some simple decoration, and its position halfway down the church is an indication that the chancel has been lengthened. In fact it happened in the thirteenth century, which explains the stepped lancets that make up the east window.

The restoration of 1903 appears to have been fairly stringent, and one of its results was a new front for the capacious west gallery; instead of the customary balustrade it was fitted with a wooden screen in the form of a close mesh. It is a skilfully-fashioned piece of joinery reflecting the influence of the 'arts and crafts' movement. Surprisingly the ceiling was left in place, although it is possible to see the rather unusual arrangement of roof timbers, consisting of tie beams with struts curving outwards to meet collar beams.

There are some interesting details in the nave. Right at the back, opposite the gallery stairs, is a small monument of 1679 to Thomas Holland with careful lettering embellished by some naive scratchings representing the emblems of

*Onibury church. The thirteenth-century chancel has single and stepped lancets and a blocked priest's door.*

death. Some seventeenth-century pews are preserved here. In the body of the nave each pew has its coat peg on the wall - a sensible arrangement possibly unique to Onibury. The pulpit, too, is intriguing, being apparently constructed in two pieces of different ages and looking fragile as a result. At some point, possibly during restoration, it was reinforced on the wall side by a couple of old box pew doors, one still bearing its number. Note the large consecration cross on the wall next to it.

The most interesting features of the long, brick-paved chancel are some uncommon monuments. The altar is flanked by two seventeenth-century floor slabs in cast iron, a rare material for memorials at this time, while on the south wall Dorothy Pytt's wall monument (1657) is an early essay in the classical style. A simple plaque is framed by roughly-cut pillars with plain capitals supporting a curious arrangement of three-balled finials.

Talking of monuments, it is pleasant to see the memorials of two former incumbents enlivened by their photographs.

## Oswestry (Christ Church)

*The church is not always open, but access can be arranged by contacting the minister at 65 Oakhurst Road, Oswestry (telephone Oswestry 658301).*

Christ Church is the only nonconformist place of worship to be included in this book, and it qualifies because the architect, W.H.Spaull, obviously intended to build a church and not a chapel. He designed it for the local Congregationalists and it was completed in 1872. In recent years it has undergone considerable refurbishment and is now used by the United Reformed Church.

The building is an excellent example of the very free style that followed the purism of the Gothic revival earlier in the century. Constructed in rock-faced masonry to suggest rugged strength, it conforms to no rules, and Spaull felt at liberty not only to mix Early English and Decorated styles but to use them without any inhibiting sense of accuracy.

He started with the advantage of a fine site. The church has a commanding position fronting the small square at the foot of the castle motte. So, unlike Oswestry's two parish churches it is an integral part of the town centre and almost literally in the market place. The facade is impressive - the result of a need to incorporate the traditional twin chapel doors and a wide entrance lobby behind them. A broad west gable contains a big five-light window with multi-foil tracery, and below it the doors are incorporated into a row of five blind arches with foliage capitals. The other three arches have small windows in a quatrefoil shape.

The north-west tower and the broach spire are very much part of the facade, in perfect proportion to the rest of the building. The tower has twin-light windows

*Victorian Gothic variations at Christ Church, Oswestry.*

and (for added variety) an arrow slit, while the spire is embellished with elongated bell openings.

The south wall presents an array of cusped lancet windows, some slender in the orthodox Early English fashion and some very fat. In the transept wall is a pair of lancets set into arches with triangular heads, and above them a large rose window with a tracery pattern of radiating leaf shapes.

These are the public sides of the church. The north and east walls are less elaborate, although the north transept has a smaller rose window.

Although Spaull was constrained by the requirements of chapel worship the interior is definitely that of a spacious and well-proportioned church. Twin two-bay arcades turning inwards at right angles suggest an Early English plan of nave, aisles and transepts without intruding on the central space. Ribs rise from corbels to support the wooden roof, now attractively painted. A broad and shallow 'chancel' is backed by a decorative blind arch and flanked on one side by a very Anglican stone and marble pulpit. At the west end a big gallery is fronted by a wooden frieze with a lancet motif.

The total effect is a pleasing mixture of Gothic detail and the classical 'auditorium' plan, and recent redecoration has imparted warmth to the interior without detracting from its dignity.

## RICHARDS CASTLE (ALL SAINTS)

*137: 495706*
*At Batchcott, 4 miles south of Ludlow on B4361.*

Richards Castle is in Herefordshire, but its church is in Shropshire - a mile away near the hamlet of Batchcott. But then churchgoing has never been easy for the residents of the present village of Richards Castle. The original settlement was centred on a Norman castle that pre-dated 1066, its owner having been invited in by Edward the Confessor to help subdue the troublesome Welsh border. Naturally the medieval church was also built here, and continued in use long after a new village grew up nearly a mile away to the south-east.

By the end of the nineteenth century St. Bartholomew's was in urgent need of restoration, and Mrs Hannah Foster, the occupant of Moor Park, the local 'big house', offered to fund it in memory of her husband and daughter. She approached Richard Norman Shaw, one of the most innovative architects of the day, to carry out the work, but was told that a new church could be built for the cost of restoring the old one. The prospect of re-siting the church must have seemed attractive to Mrs Foster because Moor Park (now a school) was a long way from St. Bartholomew's, but if the villagers hoped to get a church on their doorsteps they were disappointed. The site chosen was halfway between Moor Park and the village, so they were faced with just as long a walk.

Shaw had worked in Shropshire some years before. He designed the little church at Peplow and built Adcote, one of his most celebrated houses, near Baschurch. He was not a great enthusiast for Gothic, preferring to draw on various styles of English domestic architecture for inspiration, and when asked for a design based on the old church of St. Bartholomew he produced something very distinctive.

The site is on gently-rising ground that gives the church a commanding position when approached from the south. It is built in pale local stone that has yellowed slightly with age, and although its appearance is recognisably Gothic in the fourteenth-century style the whole outline is softened. This is particularly true of the tower, which is sturdy and impressive but with no Gothic spikiness. The result is a church which succeeds in dominating its surroundings without being aggressive.

Nowadays the main entrance is on the north side, but Shaw planned an approach leading off the road from the village and providing a formal walk to a door in the tower, which is almost detached from the church and has something of the effect of a gatehouse. The interior is unVictorian in its austerity, with a preponderance of smooth, near-white Grinshill stone in the walls and in the sweeping arcade dividing the nave from the south aisle. There is no stained glass, although the original scheme apparently provided for it, and no doubt Shaw envisaged more interior colour. As it is, the richest feature is the huge triptych over the altar, painted by George Buckeridge and strongly reminiscent of his similar work in Bromfield church. There is further fine craft work in the stalls, pews, iron chancel screen and particularly in the intricately-carved pulpit and sounding board.

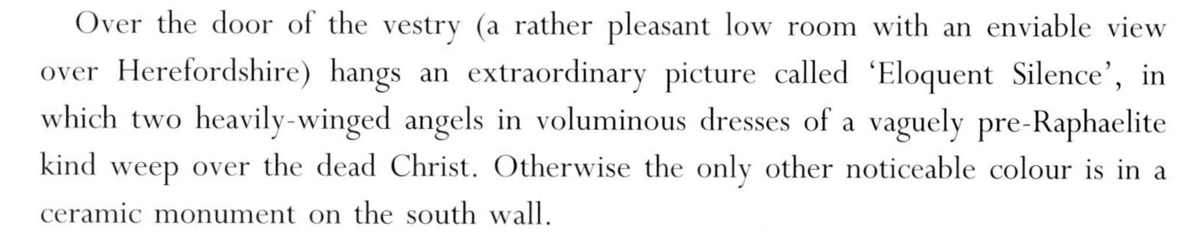

Over the door of the vestry (a rather pleasant low room with an enviable view over Herefordshire) hangs an extraordinary picture called 'Eloquent Silence', in which two heavily-winged angels in voluminous dresses of a vaguely pre-Raphaelite kind weep over the dead Christ. Otherwise the only other noticeable colour is in a ceramic monument on the south wall.

*Richards Castle: a striking essay in fourteenth-century style by Norman Shaw.*

All Saints' may well be a difficult church to love, not only because of its severity but because it lacks the accumulation of details - or clutter as it is sometimes called - that emphasise associations with its community. But it should certainly not be missed by enthusiasts for Victorian architecture, who will appreciate the unique touch that Norman Shaw brought to all his work.

## SHREWSBURY ABBEY

On its generous island site just across the English Bridge, the Abbey makes an impressive picture, but the present building is smaller than the monastic church at the height of its pre-sixteenth century splendour. Founded by Earl Roger de Montgomery less than twenty years after the Conquest, it became a powerful community and a mecca for pilgrims after the remains of St. Winefride were transported here in 1136.

As was customary in many urban monastic churches the nave was separately dedicated and used as a parish church by the local inhabitants, so after the Dissolution it remained in use while the chancel was demolished. Eighteenth-century engravings inside the church show a truncated building with substantial remains of the monastic accommodation, but these were swept away when the Holyhead road was constructed in the 1830s (the refectory pulpit survives on the other side of the road).

*Opposite: An 1823 drawing of Shrewsbury Abbey showing the ruined east end and the monastic buildings demolished shortly afterwards to make way for the Holyhead Road.*

The Abbey's appearance was further changed in the 1880s, when the noted architect J.L.Pearson carried out a painstaking restoration, the main feature of which was a new chancel.

It is well worth taking a preliminary walk around the exterior. The dominant feature is the tower, of typical Norman strength, although its upper part has the battlements, window openings and embellishments of the Perpendicular period.

The Norman west door, with its many roll-mouldings, is dwarfed by the immense seven-light window above it, an elaborate late-fourteenth century creation. Two stages of lights, one of them blind, support an interesting pattern of tracery in which intricate Decorated motifs are incorporated into the characteristic Perpendicular panels. The whole window is contained within a vast hood-mould that is extended upwards to form an ogee design pointing to a statue of King Edward III. It is rightly considered to be one of the very finest of Shropshire's church windows.

The north side of the church is of considerable interest. The north doorway in the porch is again Norman, although the woodwork is much later. If the door is open you can see within a rare Shropshire example of a stone barrel-vaulted roof of the twelfth century and another Norman doorway into the church itself. The two-storied superstructure of the porch was added in the late fourteenth century, and the sandstone now shows signs of erosion.

The nave exterior on this north side is a fascinating jumble of different building periods. The three gables on the north aisle, each with an adapted Perpendicular window, are a fanciful addition of 1729. Directly above and behind them is a row of clerestory windows - twin lights contained within broad semi-circular arches. No doubt they were intended to hint at a Norman motif, but their date is indicated by the polychrome stonework, popular in the 1860s. Above them again is a line of smaller windows inserted by Pearson in the 1880s and again reflecting the Norman style.

Further to the east are the projecting stumps of the former north transept with a small fragment of masonry still in place. Pearson had plans to rebuild the transept, but they were never carried out and the face was rather blandly filled in. Finally comes the pinker stone of Pearson's new chancel, quite austerely designed in an Early English style.

The south side is of lesser interest, although the position of the corresponding south transept is clearly marked.

The interior is best surveyed first from a rear pew, when the three main building periods become very obvious. Massive circular piers and semi-circular arches mark the old Norman nave, with the two rows of Victorian clerestory windows already noted from outside. These arcades are continued westwards in the later pointed style, with multi-stepped arches and slender shafted columns. The clerestory windows above this section were restored in severe Perpendicular style. These two-bay arcades link the old nave with the tower, which is hardly perceptible on the inside because of the soaring height of the arch that effectively opens up most of the lower tower wall. At the east end the thirteenth-century character of the Victorian chancel is summed up by the three widely-spaced lancets which serve as an east window.

The tower is the best place to start a tour of the interior because various pictures and documents are displayed to illustrate the history of the church. From the inside the west window loses some its architectural distinction, but the glowing heraldic glass is a compensation. Before you leave here it is worth noting that the name of the poet Wilfred Owen (The Manchester Regiment) appears on the war memorial on the north wall. Just around the corner in the north aisle are three tomb chests with coloured effigies (all brought from elsewhere) in the curious taste of the sixteenth century, together with a rather awkward wall monument of a century later. A Norman pillar piscina, originally used at the altar, stands nearby.

The chancel, now lying behind a modern sub-altar, is a very dignified structure with no Victorian fancies. A plain outer chancel arch, designed to blend with the Norman nave, is followed by an inner arch with roll moulding. The walls rise sheer and uncluttered, broken only by lancet windows. Pearson built two chancel chapels, using part of the former transept areas, and the one to the south is used as a Lady Chapel. The architect's obvious desire to impart monastic austerity to the chancel is oddly contradicted by his own reredos - a big and elaborately-coloured triptych that dominates the east end.

The south aisle contains some curiosities, including the supposed tomb slab of Roger de Montgomery, who ended his days in the Abbey, and some other ancient tombs, and there is curiosity value also in the font, which is said to be made from a section of Roman pillar from Viroconium.

Although restoration from the eighteenth century onwards left the Abbey with a rather bland interior with no great sense of antiquity, there is no doubt that Pearson's restrained additions deserve great respect. Nevertheless the final impression of the church is likely to be the exterior view of the tower and its magnificent west window, lending nobility to a less-than-splendid area of Shrewsbury.

## SHREWSBURY CATHEDRAL

### (THE CATHEDRAL CHURCH OF OUR LADY OF HELP OF CHRISTIANS AND ST. PETER OF ALCÁNTARA)

*Town Walls, Shrewsbury.*

Shrewsbury's Roman Catholic Cathedral was the result of the final recognition of the right of Catholics to freedom of worship. In 1850 Pope Pius IX created a hierarchy in England under Cardinal Wiseman, and a huge diocese was created to include Shropshire, Cheshire and North Wales. There was some debate over where the cathedral should be sited. Birkenhead was a much-favoured location because a large Irish Catholic population was concentrated in the area, but in 1851 the Earl of Shrewsbury offered to fund the construction of a cathedral, and this generosity may have tipped the balance in favour of Shrewsbury.

The chosen architect was the arch-apostle of the Gothic tradition, A.W.N. Pugin, but he died very soon after receiving the commission and the work was continued by his son Edward, who was only eighteen at the time. The extent to which Edward followed his father's designs is not known, but the interior seems to indicate that the young man had ideas of his own.

No.11 Belmont was acquired in 1852, and the land between the house and

*The elaborate chancel of Shrewsbury Cathedral contrasts with the austere Grinshill stone of the nave.*

Town Walls became available as a site for the cathedral. Consequently the building, although not particularly big, has a commanding position overlooking the river.

The exterior exemplifies A.W.N. Pugin's devotion to fourteenth-century Gothic, although the design, which included a tower, was never fully executed owing to the difficulty of finding a sufficiently firm foundation. The dominant feature is a roof of very steep pitch, giving an illusion of height that is reinforced by a tall bell-cote at the west end.

The windows are entirely in the Decorated style. The aisles have rows of three-light windows with a variety of curvilinear tracery. Those in the clerestory take the form of spheric triangles (a favourite fourteenth-century motif), while the east window is of seven lights surmounted by complex tracery. The rather nondescript porch is an Edwardian addition.

To anyone expecting a mysterious Gothic atmosphere the interior comes as a surprise. A.W.N. Pugin would undoubtedly have favoured a long, enclosed chancel, but instead we have something which is remarkably similar to the classical basilica plan, with a shallow chancel and twin arcades. The design may have been dictated by the need to accommodate a large congregation on a limited site, or perhaps Edward Pugin should be credited with the assertion of his own views. Whatever the reason, the interior is a very open structure comparable to those created by George Steuart or Thomas Telford sixty years before, although the arcades are scrupulously in keeping with the prevailing Gothic style, with octagonal piers, carved capitals and pointed arches.

It has to be said that the interior, incorporating a great deal of austere Grinshill stone, has no great beauty. There are interesting details to be sought out, however, including some good stained glass. The firm of Hardman and Company, ecclesiastical artists and craftsmen, was closely associated with Pugin, and their work can be seen in the east window and several minor ones. The most distinctive glass, however, is by Margaret Rope, a local woman who trained as an artist and continued as a practitioner in stained glass after becoming a nun.

Her work here dates from the 1920s and 1930s and has an attractive simplicity and calculated naivety. Her ambitious west window shows the English martyrs, and the life of St. Laurence is shown in the south sanctuary window. Also in the sanctuary is her record of the Eucharistic Congress of 1921 - probably the only stained glass window to portray a bus.

Some of the original fittings have been removed or replaced over the years, but the Gothic reredos, with four panels showing the Annunciation, the Nativity, the miracle at Cana and the Crucifixion, survives as an example of the work of Edward Pugin. The font is also to his design. The Stations of the Cross are 1950s work by Philip Lindsay-Clark.

## SHREWSBURY (ST. CHAD)

When old St. Chad's church was substantially ruined in 1788 by the collapse of its tower the site of its replacement was carefully chosen for maximum impact. The new church was designed to occupy a commanding position in an area that was developing as a wealthy and fashionable suburb, and it was inevitable that the style of the church should be fashionable too. That meant a building in the classical idiom. George Steuart was no doubt invited to submit plans on the strength of his fine work at Attingham Hall a few years before and his recently-completed church at Wellington - both in the conventional taste of the time.

His design for St. Chad's, however, was a radical innovation, controversial on its completion in 1792 and remaining so for a century afterwards. Instead of the usual rectangular basilica pioneered at Whitchurch in 1712 he stipulated a circular nave which was in effect a rotunda. A near-detached tower formed an entrance hall, which was linked to the nave by an antechamber, producing a distinctive tripartite structure.

*St. Chad's in Victorian times.*

The impressive west facade dominates the approach from Town Walls. A deep portico marks the entrance, and above it the tower rises on a square base, continuing as a polygonal bell-chamber embellished with twin pilasters and finishing as a cupola with its dome supported on tall Corinthian columns. The walls of the antechamber protrude as semi-circles and link with the nave, the two sections being unified by a balustrade. The exterior walls of the nave have a pattern of twin Ionic pilasters alternating with tall windows. It is a restrained and highly sophisticated design.

On entering the church you pass through a spacious porch into the antechamber, which houses the elegant gallery stairways. The nave reveals itself as a capacious yet

*The interior of St. Chad's, with the chancel darkened by the addition of stained glass.*

quite intimate auditorium, not quite circular because the shallow chancel recess occupies one segment. The galleries follow the sweep of the nave walls, supported on cast iron columns that are continued above the gallery to the flat plastered ceiling.

The chancel is heavily emphasised by pairs of tall Corinthian columns on each side and contains a handsomely-proportioned Venetian window. It originally contained glass by the gifted Francis Eginton but now bears a copy of a Rubens picture by the ubiquitous and less gifted local artist David Evans. (For an idea of what the original window may have looked like you need to look at the Eginton window in St. Alkmund's.)

Over the years other additions have altered the character of this simple, cool, spare interior. The reredos, which looks like seventeenth-century baroque work, was in fact installed in the early 1920s as a war memorial and portrays the Crucifixion, the Nativity and the Ascension. It fits reasonably well into Steuart's design, as does the marble bowl of the font, but the same cannot be said of the brass and copper pulpit, which is in the worst taste of the late nineteenth century.

Of the various memorials the two most interesting (and both decently restrained because they are partly the work of Francis Chantrey) are mounted on each side of the chancel. They commemorate the builder of the church, John Simpson, and the famous ironmaster William Hazledine.

## SHREWSBURY (ST. MARY'S)

*The church is now redundant. Current opening times may be obtained from the Tourist Information Centre.*

St. Mary's stands in the centre of a close on a high level site that might well have been occupied by the castle if an Anglo-Saxon church had not already claimed the position. The new Norman church was built at the end of the twelfth century in red sandstone and consisted of a nave, chancel and short transepts. It must have looked long, slender and elegant, but over the centuries it has developed (almost literally) middle-age spread. The additions and modifications, ranging in date from the early thirteenth to the nineteenth centuries, can be seen by taking a clockwise walk round the church.

The tower was a very early addition, probably the result of a decision not to build one at the transept crossing. Its base, featuring a big round-arched west door and smaller windows above, is obviously Norman, but the upper section, with a change of stone, decorative battlements, crocketed finials and a needle spire is an embellishment of two hundred years later. The same building phase also gave the church a new clerestory and a shallow-pitched roof.

The south porch underwent the same process in miniature. It was built when the north and south aisles were added, perhaps thirty years or so after the completion of the church. Its original Norman doorway survives, and there are two interesting side windows with plate tracery in a quatrefoil design that belongs to the early thirteenth century. But the upper storey of the porch has windows of both the Decorated and Perpendicular periods. Incidentally the interesting outer door of the porch was constructed from remnants of the rood screen.

If you continue the anti-clockwise circuit you will see that the south transept is hardly perceptible, having been almost engulfed when the big Trinity Chapel was added to the south-east corner of the church towards the middle of the fourteenth century. Its small Norman doorway is still there. In the corresponding position at the north-east corner a vestry was inserted fairly tactfully in 1884, but most of the original north transept can still be seen. The north porch is a late-Victorian addition.

As you enter the church the huge east window makes an immediate impact, but the first features of interest are the nave arcades. They represent the walls of the

*The south side of St. Mary's, Shrewsbury, reveals a variety of medieval styles. From the far left: the late-Norman porch with its added upper storey, the Perpendicular windows of the south aisle (inserted during fifteenth century alterations), the fifteenth century clerestory above, the original transept with stepped lancet windows and Norman doorway, and the fourteenth century Trinity chapel with Decorated windows.*

original nave, and it is easy to see that congregational space was limited, making necessary the construction of aisles at an early date. Although the arcades went up in the very early years of the thirteenth century they are quite sophisticated in design and demonstrate the transition from Norman massiveness to a more slender and decorative style, with clusters of shafts symmetrically arranged and surmounted by carved capitals. The arches, however, are still semi-circular in the old Romanesque fashion. The north arcade has the crisper and more intricate carving of the type known as stiff-leaf, with occasional interspersed heads.

Presumably a clerestory was constructed to let in light when the aisles were added. If so it was remodelled comprehensively more than two centuries later when the heavy timbers of the old pitched roof were replaced by lighter braces supporting a near-flat roof composed of carved panels with elaborate bosses that feature animals among other designs. The chancel arch is tall, pointed and entirely characteristic of the thirteenth century, but the two windows above it are unusually complex and artistic. Set within a rounded arch are twin pointed sub-arches, and the decoration echoes that of the arcades.

It is not easy now to get a sense of the church's original cruciform shape because the north transept contains the eighteenth-century organ case and the south transept is blocked off by a modern screen and inaccessible without a key. However, you can pass beneath the organ to inspect the rather complicated space beyond. Apart from the unusual cross-hatched decoration of the transept walls the most interesting feature here is the vault containing an altar. It is the remnant of a chapel which formed part of the original church design (the corresponding chapel in the south transept disappeared in the building of the Trinity chapel.) Other early work here includes the pair of splayed lancet windows.

The chancel is hardly magnificent, but there is compensation in the vast fourteenth-century Jesse window. Given its size and complexity it is astonishing to learn that it was first installed in the town's Franciscan friary, was moved in the sixteenth century to the old St Chad's, and finally came to rest here in 1792. The north wall of the chancel reveals signs of proposed modifications of uncertain date

*The interior of St. Mary's, Shrewsbury, showing two of its finest features - the nave arcades in transitional style between Norman and Early English, and the finely crafted windows in similar style above the chancel arch.*

that were never carried out - possibly a scheme to provide a matching north chapel. Also on this wall is a surprisingly sophisticated window arrangement of stepped lancets with sturdy detached shafts, apparently there to accommodate a wall passage. The chancel east wall is almost entirely Victorian in design and the south wall is hardly present, having been opened up with a generous fourteenth-century arch to supplement the rather smaller one of a century earlier.

The arches lead to the Trinity chapel, which was made over to the important Drapers' Company in 1460. It is a spacious room, and, as in the chancel, its north wall shows indications of abandoned rebuilding work which must have pre-dated the present large arched opening. There is a long and elaborate Victorian reredos, but of particular interest are the fifteenth-century carved alabaster panels set into the back of the sedilia. The big east window is Victorian, with glass of the 1840s by David Evans surrounding a centre section of 1892.

As noted previously, it is difficult to get a view of the south transept, but visible over the screen are splayed lancet windows similar to those in the north transept and a design of intersecting blind arcades, very much like the famous wall at Wenlock Priory and probably of the same late Norman date. As you walk through the arch into the south aisle note that its construction almost eliminated the small Norman window that pre-dated it.

I have not so far mentioned St. Mary's chief claim to fame - its collection of medieval European glass, assembled mainly by a mid-Victorian rector. It forms something of a treasure house, but space does not allow a detailed description here, and recourse to a church guidebook is necessary.

In terms of history St. Mary's is the equivalent of St. Laurence's at Ludlow, being a basically simple church made grander by means of later commercial wealth, but it is much less intimidating than St Laurence's. It retains a more homely scale and has an attractive air of haphazard development. Now disused, it is in the care of the Shropshire Historic Churches Trust, an organisation that deserves a generous donation because its work within the county will undoubtedly become ever more necessary.

## STANTON LACY (ST. PETER)

*137: 496788*
*3½ miles north-west of Ludlow off B4365.*

Excavations in the Bromfield and Stanton Lacy area have shown a remarkable continuity of settlement from the Bronze Age through the period of Roman occupation and into Saxon and medieval times. It was evidently a well-developed part of Shropshire, and after the the Conquest Stanton was a prosperous manor held by the de Lacy family, the original builders of Ludlow Castle. It is hardly surprising, therefore, that an ambitious Saxon church in the cruciform Mercian style should have been built here in the eleventh century.

If the church is ancient the churchyard is probably older still, showing on the south side the semi-circular shape that suggests a round enclosure housing a Celtic church (the farm has intruded to the north).

If you pause inside the churchyard gate you can get an inkling of the appearance of the original church by ignoring the lean-to addition on the south side. Like most Mercian churches it was very tall in relation to its width, and this also applied to the transepts, one of which survives on the north side. Further Saxon evidence is visible on the west wall, where lengths of pilaster strips remain. These were a characteristic form of embellishment, and they continue on the north wall of the nave and on the transept. The blocked north door to the nave is a very handsome piece of eleventh-century work, well shaped and proportioned and flanked by pilaster strips which continue over the door as a hood-mould. Continuing the walk round to the south side you can

*Stanton Lacy church. The south aisle was rather clumsily added to the Saxon nave in the fourteenth century.*

see an unusual exterior feature - a pair of tomb recesses set into the south chancel wall. Their style is of the fourteenth century but erosion has made the effigies totally unrecognisable.

If by now you anticipate entering a chaste and primitive Saxon building you will be disappointed because the interior is dominated by blinding stained glass. Most of it is by David Evans of Shrewsbury, a Victorian artist noted for what his admirers call 'glowing colour' and for what others regard as insensitive gaudiness. The perpetrator of most of it was the Revd. Joseph Bowles, vicar from 1847 until 1879, who was also responsible for an early restoration in the 1850s. He was determined to leave his mark; he appears in the guise of St. Peter in the west window and his coat of arms can be seen in the east window of the south aisle.

From the back of the church it is possible to see its components. To the left is the early nave north wall leading to the original north transept. To the right is the lean-to south aisle which becomes a kind of south transept at the tower crossing - this area, together with the tower were the result of a fourteenth-century modification. Ahead is the long thirteenth-century chancel.

At the tower crossing on the north side the tall and narrow proportions of the transept can be appreciated. In the original church the transepts would have been used as chapels rather than as a means of enlarging the accommodation, and they must have been extremely dark, being lit at best by a tiny splayed window. The present window of three stepped lancets belongs to the fourteenth century. The tower arches here are of interest in that those to the east and west have ballflower ornament, a feature of the north aisle in Ludlow church but comparatively rare in Shropshire village churches.

The chancel is long, and its twin-lancet windows date it to the thirteenth century, although one is cusped and may be a later addition. There is a good deal of Victorian work here, including the attractive little pipe organ, the violent east window (presumably Evans again), the green painted ceiling with its scattered symbols, the unusual altar and the reredos with five painted panels. These are intriguing. Representing Christ and four saints in a homely sort of way, they are obviously too modern to be standard Victorian work and the backgrounds appear to be local scenes (the church appears in one of them). Are they by a local artist? And what did they replace? Whatever the answers, these unassuming pictures do much to make up for the windows.

## STOKESAY (ST. JOHN THE BAPTIST)

*137: 435817*
*1 mile south of Craven Arms.*

Stokesay church is virtually within the grounds of the castle and most visitors look in briefly, but it is an interesting building in its own right and worth more than a cursory inspection.

In 1646 it was severely damaged during a Civil War skirmish at the castle, and a substantial rebuilding of the nave took place in 1654, making it one of the few churches in England to have received this sort of attention during Cromwell's regime. It was founded in the twelfth century in association with the first castle at Stokesay (the present fortified manor house was built in the late thirteenth century) and the tower and chancel were probably added in the fifteenth century, although they could have been adaptations of existing structures. Both were rebuilt in 1664.

The south doorway, with its big shafts and single-stepped arch, is the only feature to have survived from the Norman church. It leads into a nave that is almost entirely of the seventeenth century, and the giant texts that cover the walls are typical of the period - the Creed, the Commandments and a whole stretch of Exodus are laid out in huge, laborious script. Sensibly covered up in the eighteenth century, they were revealed in the 1870s by restorers with misguided antiquarian tastes, but they do nothing for the church interior.

*Stokesay church.*

No doubt the box pews were installed at or soon after the rebuilding, and there are two very substantial canopied versions that would have allowed the occupants to disappear from view entirely, although they have none of the special comforts that often accompany this kind of privileged seating. In fact the box pews, apart from their draughtproofing, seem to have been just as excruciating as the rough late-medieval benches under the gallery. This gallery, incidentally, would have been an eighteenth-century addition, and was constructed with some delicacy. The pulpit, with its reader's desk and sounding board is a fine piece very much in keeping with the other nave fittings. It apparently suffered when choir stalls were introduced.

A tie beam at the chancel entrance carries the date 1664 and helped to support a screen that was another victim of the choir stalls. It is painful to reflect on the damage done in many small churches by the nineteenth-century craze for moving the choir from the gallery.

*The elaborate 'gentry pews' in Stokesay church.*

But at least the chancel is not dominated by stained glass; that is found in the south windows of the nave, forming two interesting memorials. The figures of St. Michael and St. Gabriel commemorate Edward Hotchkiss of the Army Flying Corps, "the first Shropshire aviator", who died in 1902. The other window is both distinctive and charming. In a sort of Art Nouveau style it shows the summoning of the shepherds at the nativity, but instead of delivering a rousing message the angels are chatting graciously with the shepherds for all the world like two ladies from the big house who have encountered some estate workers on their walk. It is all taking place in an English landscape featuring a dry stone wall, and is a memorial to Ernest Tredinnick, who joined the army as a trooper, served in the Boer War and was commissioned from the ranks.

# TONG (ST. BARTHOLOMEW)

*127: 795074. 4 miles east of Shifnal on A41.*

Splendidly exposed, and dominating the view from the A41, St. Bartholomew's presents a standing invitation to stop, stare and investigate. It is the best example in the county of a complete Perpendicular church, and there is probably no other Shropshire church that makes such an immediate impact on the casual passer-by.

*Tong church, highly embellished in the Perpendicular style.*

The eye is drawn at once to the octagonal central tower with its abbreviated

spire, but the other characteristics of the Perpendicular period are a forcefully present - the fine array of stylised battlements and pinnacles, the low-pitched roof with gargoyles, the integral south porch and the window tracery. It speaks of wealth and is certainly no humble village church.

Elizabeth, widow of the lord of the manor Sir Fulke Pembrugge, built the church in 1410 as a collegiate foundation with a warden and four priests, whose tasks were to say Masses for her three husbands and to sustain thirteen poor people. Its subsequent history as a parish church is closely bound up with the Vernon and Durant families who later occupied Tong castle. (The castle was rebuilt in the eighteenth century but demolished in 1954.) These family links are emphasised by the astonishing array of monuments which can easily distract attention from the interior itself.

The austere nave has north and south aisles, and the Perpendicular style is apparent in the near-flat roof with ribs and bosses, the generous windows and the very tall arches of the arcades with their octagonal piers. Characteristically the arches have little embellishment beyond simple chamfers. The carved wooden chancel screen is original - unemphatic in itself but marking a definite boundary between secular and sacred. Thanks to sympathetic restoration in the 1890s it is possible even today to sense the more rarified atmosphere of the chancel, where the daily offices would have been said by the college of priests. Their stalls survive, not totally original but retaining rather formal misericords and looking venerable (an impression reinforced by the riot of names and initials carved on them, although these are presumably the work of later choirboys).

The big east window has five lights divided by a transom, enabling the artist to portray ten saints, and saints appear again on the reredos in the form of figures carved at Oberammagau. This is Victorian work, but the sedilia and piscina are original. The wall monument above the sedilia commemorates Ann Wylde, who died in 1624 at the age of sixteen shortly after the birth of her child, and is an early example of the new classical taste. The figure is homely - almost Elizabethan - but the surround is severely architectural, with Corinthian columns supporting an

*Opposite: Elaborate tombs in front of the Vernon chapel at Tong.*

entablature and a coat of arms. But historically the most interesting features of the sanctuary are the modern reproductions of 'houselling benches', the flat-topped rails that were in use before Archbishop Laud specified the more familiar kind of communion rail in the early seventeenth century.

Opinions differ concerning the aesthetic qualities of the large chest tombs in the nave and south transept. They are certainly obtrusive and detract from our appreciation of a fine interior, but such a rich collection of craftsmanship in the late medieval tradition is a rare and fortunate survival in a village church. In most cases there is as much pleasure to be gained from the carving on the chest surrounds as from the conventional effigies above. There is little point in describing each in detail here since the booklet obtainable in the church does it so well, in addition to telling the interesting stories of those commemorated.

The 'Golden Chapel' in the

south aisle, however, cannot be passed over. It is a small room, separated from the body of the church by an ogee-headed door and by a flattened arch with the tomb of Sir Henry Vernon (died 1515) beneath it. The arch itself bears four niches (the headless figures which occupy them were taken from an adjacent tomb) each surmounted by a richly-carved canopy. The tomb chest is finely embellished by panels containing figures and heraldic devices alternately. The striking feature of the chapel interior is the fan-vaulting of the roof - rare in Shropshire, and executed here with great sophistication. Under the carpet and set into medieval tiles is an unusual brass showing a tonsured Arthur Vernon (died 1516) in academic dress, while a bust of him holding a book rests on a bracket on the west wall. An elaborate canopy is carved above.

*The unusual sixteenth-century bust of Sir Arthur Vernon at Tong.*

The two-tiered tomb in front of the chapel was apparently moved here from the sanctuary by George Durant, who wanted his own memorial to occupy the prime position. Durant was the wealthy 'nabob' who bought Tong Castle in 1760 and at once proceeded to build a replacement in the 'Gothick' style fashionable in some circles at the time. Whether this nouveau-riche regime was popular in the village is not known - the church guide tells us in deadpan fashion that George's son *"stamped his very eccentric personality on the area... He had 32 illegitimate children in the village of Tong."* Be that as it may, George Durant's memorial ended up in a less than prominent position inside one of the crossing piers. It is a conventional late-eighteenth century piece showing a woman in classical draperies and with one breast bared grieving beside a funeral urn.

As you leave the church do not miss the Victorian instructions in the porch for the ringing of the Great Bell of Tong. When it came to according this honour the long-established local landowners and the vicar were given equal status with royalty - a seemly piece of rural diplomacy.

## WHITCHURCH (ST.ALKMUND)

St Alkmund's is a church of great architectural significance for Shropshire, although it is the result of a fortunate accident. Pictures of its predecessor survive and show a conventional medieval church with a later central tower in the style of the fifteenth century. It was this tower that collapsed in 1711. Disasters of this kind were not unusual, but they seldom led to a complete rebuilding; the decision to embark on a brand new church meant that Whitchurch pioneered a provincial version of the style introduced by Wren and his London colleagues only a few years before.

With its rectangular plan and its twin arcades it is designed in the Roman 'basilica' form derived from Italian models, although it lacks the flamboyance characteristic of Wren's London churches. It was not in fact the work of an architect but of a firm of stonemasons - William and Richard Smith of Tattenhall in Staffordshire - who must have worked from one of the early 'pattern books' of architectural drawings which were beginning to circulate in the provinces.

The exterior has features unprecedented in Shropshire in 1712. The round-headed windows are huge, and their original clear glass would have flooded the church with light, removing all Gothic mystery. The slender tower is not a separate component but an integral part of the symmetrical west facade. The building is embellished with classical balustrades, replacing the battlements of the Perpendicular period. The south porch is semi-circular. The overall effect is one of restrained elegance.

*St. Alkmund's, Whitchurch: an early view from the south.*

The interior has undergone considerable changes, and it is worth spending a few minutes in a mental reconstruction of the original. The choir stalls and fine organ, for example are intrusions. The first organ would have been in the west gallery, and the stalls were not put in until the 1880s. Together with the Edwardian lady chapel they form a chancel that was not envisaged in the Smith brothers' plan. (The side walls indicate that no structural break existed between nave and sanctuary.) The area they occupy would have accommodated a towering 'three-decker' pulpit and no doubt some large box pews for the gentry.

Marks on the arcade columns show where the timbers of the north and south galleries were clamped to them until 1972, and the structural method can still be seen in the surviving west gallery. The stained glass is another nineteenth-century

*St. Alkmund's, Whitchurch, from the north.*

innovation; impressive though it is, it detracts from the original concept of an interior bathed in clear white light. The reredos is even later, although its Corinthian pilasters are very much in keeping with the spirit of the original church.

None of these changes affects the basic revolutionary design of the interior, intended to be an auditorium in which the dignified sanctuary with its triple windows and Corinthian pilasters was a stage close to, and in full sight of, the congregation. The removal of the side galleries was a great improvement aesthetically, enhancing the classical elegance of the tall Tuscan columns and round arches of the arcades, and the plasterwork of the ceilings has been beautifully restored. The chandeliers are original, and so presumably is the fine wooden structure of fluted columns and entablature that forms the doorway to the vestry at the west end.

Considering the growing interest in architecture among Shropshire landowners during the eighteenth century it is surprising that this magnificent building did not immediately inspire a series of classical churches within the county. In fact it was another seventy years before George Steuart and Thomas Telford produced comparable buildings, and the sophisticated St Chad's in Shrewsbury serves to emphasise the early achievement of the obscure Smith brothers.

## WISTANSTOW (HOLY TRINITY)

*137: 433857*
*2 miles north of Craven Arms off A49.*

For regular travellers on the A49 Wistanstow is a familiar name on a signpost north of Craven Arms. Turn off the road and you find an unobtrusive village beside a long, straight lane that goes nowhere in particular. Right in the middle is the compact and stubby church, unusually symmetrical because it has twin transepts and the nave is virtually the same length as the chancel.

A small cruciform church of this kind, built all of a piece towards the end of the twelfth century, is rare in Shropshire - transepts in country churches were more often a means of later expansion - and the building is an excellent example of the Transitional architecture that retained Norman features while foreshadowing the early Gothic developments of the thirteenth century.

Unfortunately the nineteenth century has something to answer for here. Your first impression of the nave interior is likely to be of a child's laboured drawing of stonework, because the Victorian restorers followed the popular practice of scraping away the plaster of centuries to reveal the masonry. Scrupulous pointing was then used to outline every single stone. In theory the result was intended to be authentic; in practice it gives the appearance of extreme artificiality.

However, ignoring this (and the rather awful glass in the west window) there are several points of interest in the nave. It has lancet windows, very up-to-date when the church was built, and at the west end doorways on each side of the church were brutally inserted into them. They were obviously a later development, and the likelihood is that they replaced a single west door. It has been suggested that this west doorway was reconstructed to serve as a priest's door in the south wall of the chancel, and indeed the exterior of the doorway in that position is rather ornate for its humble purpose. Two other windows in the nave have been

*The cruciform church at Wistanstow. The top of the tower is probably an eighteenth-century addition.*

given stained glass representing St. Anne and St. Wistan, obviously by the same artist and of fairly modern date.

The seventeenth-century nave roof is a striking feature with alternate tie and collar beams, three tiers of wind braces in quatrefoil shapes and bosses which have been gilded in recent years.

At the tower crossing the pews give way to capacious box pews that continue into the transepts. The north transept appears to have been built first, since it has round-arched, splayed windows of the characteristic Norman type. The big north window is a fourteenth-century addition. The windows of the south transept are all in the newer pointed style. The dominant features here are the huge painted texts, dating from the seventeenth century and very similar to those at nearby Stokesay - almost certainly the work of the same craftsman. They are another rather dubious benefit of restoration.

The chancel retains its three original lancets in the east wall and there is another on the north side, but the south wall has a large, clear window of the fourteenth century, a time for letting in light. The chancel itself was redesigned in the 1960s - whether successfully or not is a matter of taste. The effect in the sanctuary of pale wood, pale stone and a pale carpet is distinctly bland, and one feels the lack of a focal point of colour.

It is worth walking round to the south chancel door before you go. It would certainly be worthy of a principal entrance, with its ornamental hood-mould ending in two heads and its single shafts supporting capitals embellished with an animal head and foliage.

# Glossary of Architectural Terms Used in the Book

Apse: a semi-circular or polygonal extension at the east end of a chancel.

Arcade: a series of arches supported on piers, usually forming a division between the nave and an aisle. Arches attached to a wall as a form of decoration are known as a blind arcade.

Ashlar: a style of masonry consisting of carefully-cut rectangular blocks of uniform dimensions and with a smooth surface.

Aumbrey: a recess or cupboard in the sanctuary designed to hold the Communion vessels.

Ballflower: a form of carved decoration popular in the early fourteenth century and resembling a ball surrounded by three petals.

Barrel vault: a semi-circular arched roof.

Basilica: a form of classical church plan providing a shallow, open chancel and a nave in which twin arcades produce spacious aisles.

Beakhead decoration: a typical Norman carved motif resembling a row of bird heads with prominent beaks.

Belfry: the part of the tower in which the bells are hung.

Bellcote: a small structure on the west end of a roof designed to hold a single bell.

Boss: a decorative feature applied at the intersection of ribs in a stone or wooden roof.

Buttress: an external structure built to reinforce a section of wall subject to lateral thrust from, for example, a roof member or arch inside the church.

Capital: the top section of a pier, usually wider than the pier itself and embellished with moulding or carving.

Chamfered arch: an arch in which the sharp right-angles of the masonry have been cut to provide an angled edge.

Chancel: the eastern section of a church or chapel containing the sanctuary and often the choir stalls as well.

Chancel arch: an arch marking the division between nave and chancel.

Chantry chapel: a small side chapel originally built for the purpose of saying Masses for the soul of a dead person.

Chevron decoration: a zig-zag motif most often found in Norman doorways.

Cinquefoil: see 'foil'

Clerestory: a row of windows set at the top of the nave wall, usually introduced to provide light after the construction of a lean-to aisle.

Corbel: a block of stone projecting from a wall, either as a form of decoration or as a means of supporting a roof rib or other feature. A corbel table is a row of such blocks below the eaves of a church, a form of Norman decoration.

Crocket: a carved leaf motif used to decorate spires and pinnacles - commonly found on churches of the Decorated and Perpendicular periods.

Crossing: the intersection of nave and transepts in a cruciform church. It often lies beneath the tower.

Cusped: see 'foil'.

Dogtooth ornament: a form of Norman carved decoration resembling a row of four-pointed stars.

Fan-vaulting: a method of roof construction by which the roof is supported on ribs rising and fanning away from a series of reinforced points (corbels) at the top of the wall.

Foil: derived from the French *feuille* (leaf) the term is used to describe the near-circular or leaf shapes used in window tracery. Foils are arranged in groups - for example a quatrefoil is a group of four resembling a four-leafed clover. A trefoil is a group of three, a cinquefoil a group of five etc. The points between the foils are called 'cusps'.

Frieze: a carved or painted strip, often seen beneath the battlements of Perpendicular towers.

Herringbone: a kind of masonry peculiar to the Saxon and early Norman periods. Rows of thin stones were set on edge, leaning to right or left in alternate courses to form a zig-zag pattern.

Hood-mould: a narrow projecting moulding above an arch or window. On the exterior it had the function of draining off rain, but it was also used inside to unify a group of windows or to accentuate the shape of an arch. Sometimes known as a dripmould or label.

Lancet: a narrow pointed window typical of the Early English period.

Misericord: a flap beneath the seat of a hinged choirstall which provided a form of seat for relief during long periods of standing. The word is sometimes applied to the entertaining carving that can be found beneath some choirstalls.

Mullions: vertical members dividing a window into separate lights.

Nook-shaft: a thin, circular moulding set within the right-angle of a piece of masonry - usually in windows or door jambs of the Norman and Early English periods.

Parclose screen: a screen closing off a side chapel - usually elaborately carved.

Pediment: A feature in the form of a shallow triangle, usually found over doors and windows in classical buildings.

Pier: a strong masonry column used to support structural weight - seen most frequently supporting the arches of arcades.

Pilaster: in classical churches a feature designed to look like a round or square column sunken into the surrounding masonry.

Pilaster strip: a vertical strip of projecting masonry used in Saxon churches to relieve the blankness of exterior walls. The more substantial early Norman version is known as a pilaster buttress.

Piscina: a basin normally set into the south wall of the sanctuary and used for washing the Communion vessels.

Quatrefoil: see 'foil'

Reredos: a decorated screen in wood or stone immediately behind the altar.

Rood loft: a structure set on a rood screen, forming a gallery.

Rood screen: a screen in wood or stone dividing the nave from the chancel and originally carrying a 'rood' or cross.

Rose window: a circular window with tracery radiating from the centre.

Rubble masonry: stones of varying size and shape not laid in regular courses.

Rustication: the term covers various decorative effects in masonry, for example texturing the face of smooth stone with a chisel, marking the mortar joints between rectangular stones in exaggerated fashion, and leaving a rough face on otherwise squared blocks. The latter is sometimes known as rock-faced masonry.

Sanctuary: the area of the chancel within the communion rails.

Sedilia: a group of seats (normally three) set against or into the south wall of the sanctuary and intended for the use of priests and deacons.

Sheila-na-gig: a pagan fertility figure, usually female, sometimes found on the exterior walls of churches of Saxon origin.

Splayed window: a means of maximising the light from a small window by cutting away the surrounding masonry at an angle. Saxon windows were 'double-splayed', ie splayed inside and out, while Norman windows had a single splay on the inside.

Stiff-leaf: a decoration consisting of stylised carved foliage.

String course: a narrow projecting band of masonry set horizontally into a wall to help break up a large blank surface.

Three-decker pulpit: an elaborate structure popular in the eighteenth century and consisting of a reading desk at ground level, a clerk's stall above it and a pulpit at the top. The pulpit usually had a 'tester' or sounding-board above it.

Tomb-chest: a monument shaped like a large chest and often bearing one or more recumbent effigies.

Transept: a sideways extension of a church at the junction of nave and chancel, designed to increase space for the congregation.

Trefoil: see 'foil'.

Tympanum: the space between the top of a door and the arch above it.

Voussoirs: wedge-shaped stones used to form a rounded arch.

# Further Reading

There are many books on church architecture, but references to Shropshire are scanty. One of the more useful is ***Local Styles of the English Parish Church*** by Sir William Addison (Batsford 1982), which discusses regional variations in church building. For newcomers to the subject I strongly recommend a study of the catalogue of Shire Publications (Cromwell House, Church Street, Princes Risborough HP27 9AJ), which contains a range of short and inexpensive books on churches and their fittings.

The first analytical study of Shropshire churches was by D.H.S. Cranage in ***An Architectural Account of the Churches of Shropshire***, published in 1903. Like all pioneering studies it is fallible, but it is a formidable and elegant work of scholarship. Copies are not easy to come by, but it can be studied in the Local Studies collection of the County Library in Shrewsbury.

The Shropshire volume of Nikolaus Pevsner's celebrated ***Buildings of England*** series (Penguin) has not been revised since the first edition in 1958, but it contains at least a mention of every church in the county at that time. Once the subject of adulation, Pevsner's work is now experiencing a rather hostile backlash, and it has to be said that his verdicts are sometimes capricious, especially on the Victorian period. (Many Victorian churches are identified but not described.) Nor is Pevsner's jumpy, idiosyncratic approach easy for beginners; it assumes considerable knowledge on the part of the reader. Nevertheless, as a comprehensive reference book it remains invaluable.

M. Salter's ***The Old Parish Churches of Shropshire*** (Folly Publications 1988) is a conscientious work in handy paperback form. As the title implies, it does not venture in detail beyond the seventeenth century, and its mechanical style and typescript format are rather forbidding, but it is a useful reference book and its church plans are a definite asset.